Anyone can do miracles!

A devotee acquires some supernatural powers by virtue of his firm devotion to his desired deity and on the strength of these powers he can work some miracles for which human intellect fail to find any earthly explanation.

A yogi, by means of his practice gets knowledge of future events and knowledge of his past births. He is freed from hunger and thirst. He can walk on water and can float in the air. He can make his body as light as cotton and can thereby walk in the air.
He can make his body as minute as an atom and can make his body gigantic. Similarly he can make it very heavy or very light. He exercises his dominion over all the elements.

The author has experienced many of such miracles presented in this book.

SAINTS
KNOWN TO ME

THE TRUE, MYSTERIOUS ANECDOTES
about unknown saints and sages from British India

D. M. KHER

VIHANG

First published in India in December 2012 by
Vihang Publications
Global edition: 14 October, 2013
ISBN: 978-81-88885-41-1

Copyright © 2012 by Rajendra Kher

All rights reserved for this edition with publisher except for use in review, the reproduction or utilization of this work in whole or in part in any form by any electronic, mechanical or other means now known or hereafter invented, is forbidden without the written permission of the publisher.

 Vihang Publications
6, Mitranand Society, Off: B. D. Kher
Squre, Anand Nagar Sinhgad Road
Pune - 411051. India.
Tel: 020-24358258
vihangpublications@gmail.com

www.vihangpublications.com

*To my revered father and mother,
who enhanced my religious mind-set*

Preface

I am now ninety years of age. By the Almighty God's grace all my senses are working well as they did in my youth. The greatest goal of man's life is salvation- union of the individual soul with the universal soul.

The fact that, whence a man comes before he takes his birth and whereto he goes after the end of his life is unknown to him. He is in complete darkness in respect of this fact. But that are omniscient who know their past births and try to avoid future ones. Such saints though rare have appeared on earth from time to time. They by their advice kept those that came in contact with them, on right path and showed them the way to salvation. In this small book I have given the lives of the saints known to me.

Even a common observer marks that a child loves light from its nativity. When it lights, it smiles in joy. Other creatures also are delightful in light. Moths and other feathered insects fly on open flames of lamps. They do so at the cost of their lives. Such is their keen love for light. In the case of birds also we observe that they fly to the east at sunrise and to the west about sunset, showing thereby that they have a natural tendency to fly in the direction of light.

Man also exerts to get himself enlightened by acquisition of knowledge.

Even in my ripe old age at present I run after light of knowledge. When I take a retrospective view of bygone years of my life, my mind takes a pause at moments when I came across saints who are enlightened personages. I yet fully remember the mystic events which I either saw or about which I heard from the most reliable persons. I remember them since I was three or four years old. My memory is not dimmed or impaired in the least.

From my childhood I had been hearing stories of saints. The mystic occurrences in their lives had left a deep impression on my mind, and confirmed my faith. This faith has dispelled all doubts and fears from my mind. It is faith which unites man with God. I fully rely upon the words of Sri Krishna that he bears the burden of protecting his devotees and that his devotees never perish. There had been a number of occasions when I experienced the truth of his word.

When I was in English school or college I read *'Sri Guru Charitra'* a number of times. This was, I must admit done with the object of earthly gain. Till I was 14, it was not settled that I should worship a particular deity. When I entered a temple in which any form of god was installed I made a reverential bow to that form, be it Ram, Vishnu, Ganesh or any other one.

But a time came when I got the chance of fixing a God for my worship. My father was *phadnis*—Public Officer—in Pune District, I was then fourteen. One day we friends were throwing stones up in the air for seeing whose stone goes higher. I picked up a stone from the ground with a view to throw it up in the air. Its touch to my fingers felt very soft. I washed it clean, and I came to know that it was not an ordinary piece of stone but the best carved image of the God Sri Ganesh. The image was carved out of a red marble. All the details were beautifully carved out in that marble which was ¾ inch by ½ inch. The image had a crown and four hands. In its two hands there were a noose and a goad. On its navel was carved the hood of a cobra. I was immensely delighted by the acquisition of that charming image.

When my father came home from his office in the evening I showed that image to him. He was right glad to see it. On the 4th day of the dark fortnight of that month the image was installed with due rites and we then began to worship it from that time. I was inclined to worship Sri Ganesh and in course of time I became a staunch devotee of Sri Ganesh.

Before my thread ceremony my father had taught me *sandhya*—a prayer performed at the time of sunrise—without *Gayatri* mantra, *purushasukta, sri sukta* and *Ganapati atharvashirsha*. After thread ceremony I regularly used to repeat them everyday. Time allowing, I used to repeat the *Ganapati atharvashirsha* many times. I found thereby a benevolent change in my career.

While I was in college, my father advised me to mutter a certain mantra for propitiating the God Ganapati. At the same time he had led down certain rules of conduct for my guidance. Since then I have been strictly observing them until now. I have derived many benefits by acting upto the advice of my father. By means of propitiation, my mind has become quite calm and carefree. With all this I have not forsaken my necessary duties.

Having had great faith in matters divine, I had a keen desire to enjoy the sweet company of saintly persons. That desire has also been fulfilled by the Almighty God. I was associated for a long time with the devotees of yogis like Kaka Puranik, Keshavrao Yeolekar, Sarange *Sanyasi* and Bhapkar *Maharaj*. I received information about other saints from my respected father and elder brother. The information is true and correct as it is based on perfectly sound evidence. It is difficult to satisfy those who are prone to disbelieve indirect evidence. In respect of such persons what else is in my hands than to make a bow to them to satisfy them.

Mystic events and miracles are beyond the scope of physical science. From times immemorial such events have uptil now taken place in India. To prove the veracity of such instances I may note some of them hereunder. Sri Ram was on Southwards journey for the purification of his wife Sita. On his way there were some yogis in invisible form under the tree. Sri Ram is described as having hugged them. Hanuman is described as having brought the Dronagiri mountain when Lakshman had become unconscious, owing to his having been attacked by a deadly missile. This very Hanuman assumed a tiny form & handed over Sri Ram's ring to Sita in the Ashoka forest. Sri Krishna on the strength of his 'Satya' and 'Dharma' revived the life of Abhimanyu. Similarly Sri Krishna showed his 'Vishwarupa' to Arjuna when he was bewildered in respect of his duty. Sri Vithal assumed the form of Mahar and in that garb paid money into the treasury of Bijapur and freed Damaji from dire consequences. Sri Dnyaneshwar made a he-buffalo to recite Veda like a human being. He made an earthen wall walk and gave life to Satchidanandababa who was dead. Namdeo made the God of stone eat food offered to him. Eknath brought the deceased fathers of the Brahmins to eat food on the day of *shraadha*—day of remembrance of the deceased—because the Brahmins had refused to take it on some technical ground. Saint Tukaram went to heaven on the back of Garuda. Sri Narsimha Saraswati of Ganagapur assumed several like forms resembling himself and paid visit to the abodes of different devotees on the Diwali holiday. Ramakrishna Paramahamsa, when he visited the 'Kali' Temple he saw the living image of 'Kali' and not the stone image. Swami Vivekananda lost all his senses as soon as he was touched by a finger of Ramakrishna. He went into a trance and become a great yogi. Vasudevananda Saraswati, while roaming by the side of the Narmada river, flew into the sky and appeared before his devotees. Another saint on the bank of Narmada river is reported to have brought water of that river and turned it into Ghee for serving it at the time of dinner.

None can doubt or say that the above events are false. When man's mind is highly developed to its utmost degree such mystic events actually do take place. It has also its own science. The miracles take place according to certain rules. There is nothing strange in them as they occur according to certain rules of nature which are generally unknown to a common man.

In this book, short lives of some saints are given. Out of these Hariboa and Bhapkar Maharaj were Yogis. Bindu Madhav Puranik was one on whom Sri Datta had conferred his favours. Similarly, Baba Vaikar was a devotee of Sri Datta. Bindu Madhav alias Kaka Puranik began to recite Purana at once without previous study of Sanskrit language. Sarange Sanyasi who was a block head till he was twelve or thirteen years old at once began to make *kirtan*—presenting cultural stories along with holy songs—like an expert *kirtankaar*. This is all indeed most wonderful. Physical science cannot offer plausible explanation of these wonderful facts.

I had close contact with Kaka Puranik for about ten years. I got information about Baba Vaikar from Kaka Puranik and about Kau Akkaa from my elder brother. I had been associated with Bhapkar Maharaj at Karjat in Ahmednagar District for about fourteen years. Sarange Sanyasi used to see my father every year at Pune. This he did for three successive years. I was then a boy of ten or eleven years of age. Keshavboa Yevalekar annually paid his visit to us at Jamkhed. I had contact with him for nearly twelve years. I also used to see my brother's Guru Vyankat Shastri Dravid off and on, for nearly six years.

The Almighty wished to enlarge himself एकोऽहं बहुःस्याम् and he created the universe. Its creation and his entry therein were simultaneous actions. Man's body also contains a portion of this greatest power. If a man knows and develops this power, he can make wonderful acts by virtue of this power. There is an old saying that if a man exerts he can achieve the powers of God Naaraayana. *upaasanaa*—rituals, *bhakti*—devotion and *dnyaana*—self-knowledge are the ways to achieve that power. Although these ways are different, their ultimate goal is the same. Men may follow any of these ways; they must reach the common goal. However, they must take the help of Yoga for accomplishing their object. *dhaaranaa* and *dhyaana* are necessary even in the case of *Bhakti* or *dnyaana*. Without *dharana* and *dhyana* man cannot reach the state of *samadhi* and without *samadhi* union with the Supreme Soul is impossible.

As Yogis get certain *siddhis*—spiritual powers— so also, those who follow *bhakti, upasana* or *dnyana* get some similar powers. In yoga, *ahimsa*—non-violence, satya—following the truth, *asteya, brahmacharya*—celibacy and *aparigriha*—desire-lessness are 'yamas' and purity, satisfaction, penance, study of sacred books and worship of God, are the 'niyamas.' These *yamas* and *niyamas*, if tenaciously practiced, bring certain *siddhis* to those who practice them.

Man who strictly follows the rules of Ahimsa creates an atmosphere of Ahimsa round about him. Take for instance the Ashram of Vasishtha Rishi or the Ashram of Jabali Muni, even the animals in those Ashrams had forgotten their natural antipathy.

I have given in this book an instance in which Vithoba Anna Karhadkar took out a thorn from a tiger's foot. This he did on the strength of the above principle. In the open space in front of the Avaliya baba of the village Chilavdi, various animals having natural antipathy were playing and behaving with one another like intimate friends.

If a man goes on observing a vow of ever telling the truth the result is that his word becomes true. If he says that a certain circumstance will take place, it actually takes place without any efforts. Similarly if a yogi makes a vow to abstain from stealing another man's property, he is provided with things though he does not wish to obtain them.

Owing to purification of mind it becomes tranquil and fit for concentration. It keeps the senses under control and this state of things makes a man fit to self uplift. Contentment gives a yogi the best happiness and God satisfies all his wants. Penance removes impurities in the body and the senses. And the yogi thereby obtains certain *siddhis* of body and senses.

A yogi, by means of his practice gets knowledge of future events and knowledge of his past births. He is freed from hunger and thirst. He can walk on water and can float in the air. He can make his body as light as cotton and can thereby walk in the air.

He can make his body as minute as an atom and can make his body gigantic. Similarly he can make it very heavy or very light. He exercises his dominion over all the elements.

These are some of the *siddhis* which a yogi obtains by several exercises in yoga.

Bindu Madhav alias Kaka Puranik, by favour of Sri Datta remembered that he was adept in reciting Purana and he began to recite it in Belbag, a temple in Pune, when he was thirteen years old. He did it without any study of Sanskrit in his present birth. Sarange Sanyasi began to make *kirtans* at the age of twelve or thirteen without any study of Sanskrit or singing. This abrupt change in his life was due to his coming into contact with a great Saint Gopalboa Vaikar. God is ever at the back of his keen devotee. Baba Vaikar's father had not a penny with him to celebrate the Navaratra festival of God Khandoba. But the God in the garb of one 'Martandrao' supplied the necessary money for that purpose. Abajiboa Puranik handed over all his belongings to the Bhillas—a tribe of thugs—in Satpuda mountain, but he was all calm and quiet. The Bhillas therefore returned all his property and paid to him Rs.1001 in addition. It was the prowess of Mantra owing to which Baba Vaikar had actual sight of God Sri Datta every day. When he lost his way in the jungle while going to Sri Shailya it was God in the form of an eagle brought him to the right path. Kau Akkaa had a power of knowing what would happen in future and she therefore had prevented my brother from taking an evening walk. My brother came to know the reason why she so prevented him when a raid of nearly one hundred and fifteen dacoits came on the village of Gangapur. Kau Akkaa had obtained this knowledge by means of her devotion to God Sri Datta. Yashwantrao Maharaj otherwise known as Dev Mamledar had acquired *siddhi* on the strength of *Ishwar pranidhan*—faith in God. My father's Guru-Yadneshwar Dixit removed the vile leprosy of his wife on the strength of a Mantra to propitiate the Goddess at Saptashrengi. Vyankatshastri Dravid—my brother's Guru had acquired *siddhi* by propitiating the Goddess 'Amba'. He thereby told my brother the exact date of his appointment as a teacher in the Elphinstone High School Bombay. He had also told Mr. Panse, a teacher in the Pune New English School, the exact dates when he will receive the amounts which he had lent to his relative and which were not forthcoming in spite of demands. Ganapatiboa Mhaskar practiced penance at Morgaon and acquired *siddhi* whereby he became free from his poverty.

Bhapkar Maharaj was an expert yogi. He could sit on water, float in the air and do many other wonderful acts.

Hariboa of Phaltan was also a yogi of the first order and by means of his various powers he also made wonderful acts. He was locked up in a shop at Tembhurni but he disappeared from it, the lock remaining intact. He was imprisoned in a jail but appeared before the police Guard as soon as the police turned his back towards the prison door. He showed that feat even to the officers of the jail, in whose presence he was locked up in the prison room. Hariboa once enlarged his body and assumed a giant like form whereby Vishudas Naagar got terrified and fell to the ground senseless. He also made lame boys walk straight. In short his life is full of mystic occurrences.

I have given lives of certain saints and the mystic powers they possessed. Owing to these powers people used to gather round them. These saints never cheated any one; they never expected to get anything from any one. On the other hand they themselves were useful to those that approached them. They left this world leaving their fame behind.

Before concluding this foreword I think that a hint to the readers is deemed necessary. There are some persons who produce sweet meats and other things on the strength of *saabari* mantras and owing to it they pass on as saints in the general public. Sometimes these *mantriks* assume the airs of saints. Producing things on the strength of yogic powers and producing them on the strength of *saabari* mantras are quite different matters. Yogis, devotees aim at salvation, not so the persons who work miracles on the strength of *saabari* mantra's. People should not mistake them to be saints. With this view I have appended one chapter at the end of this book in which I have described the wonderful acts of such *mantriks*.

I hope this small book will be useful to those who have faith in God and Mystic actions of saints.

D. M. Kher
Pune, 23rd April 1964

Publisher's Note

The first edition of this unique book was published exactly 52 years back i.e. on 21st October 1960. Due to many reasons the next edition could not be published until December 2012. It's a great honour and opportunity for us to publish this book which received quality reader.

Dattatray Mahadev alias D. M. Kher is my grandfather in-law, father of my father in-law late B. D. Kher. Both father and son had a thing in common. They kept themselves busy till the age of ninety. Both of them kept penning meaningful books till the age of ninety. Longevity is a blessing and to be able to work your favorite work is an added blessing. Like son the father too had same opportunity. D. M. Kher was a practicing lawyer. He practiced law for fifty one years. After retiring at the age of eighty six, he took a pen for good. Within a span of just a year he wrote ten books which were then immediately printed and published. When he reached ninety years of his age he had eighteen books to his credit. He mostly wrote biographies on many known-unknown saints of his time.

Because of his dedication and hard work we have got a

chance to publish such a wonderful book and the readers have a chance to read it.

As this book is written in the year 1960 the mention of time and year should be considered accordingly. For example, the writer has written, 'I can still remember the incidents occurred 78 years ago as it is.' That means we should go back to the year 78+52.

Late Mr. D. M. Kher was basically a very pious person. In addition he had many personal experiences as regards to the saints and sages. So it is but obvious that from the mines of self experience the precious gems of saints have come out.

Vihang would definitely like to publish all these worthy writings of Late Mr. D. M. Kher.

Seemantini Kher
Vihang Publications

Contents

YOGIS AND DEVOTIES

    Bindumadhav Puranik - *25*
    Baba Vaikar - *37*
    Sarange Sanyasi - *51*
    Hariboa of Phaltan - *61*
    Bhapkar Maharaj - *83*

GALAXY OF SAINTS

    Ganapati Mhaskar - *105*
    Yadneshwar Dikshit - *111*
    Apayya Dikshit - *117*
    Vyankatshastri Dravid - *119*
    Avaliya of Chilavadi - *125*
    Sheikh Mohammad - *131*
    Mamdya Vedaa - *135*
    Keshavboa Yevalekar - *137*
    Dev Mamledar - *141*
    Vithoba Anna Karhadkar - *147*

APPENDIX

    Kashirao Baba - *151*
    Jaglya of Bhingar - *155*
    Mehetar of Daund - *156*
    The Mantrik - *158*

YOGIS AND DEVOTIES

Kaka Puranik

Will you not be struck with wonder if I tell you that a boy who was of thirteen years of age and who had no knowledge of Sanskrit began to recite Puranas, Mahabharata, Bhagwat and other Puranas in Sanskrit language? Perhaps you may not even believe it! But rest assured it is a fact.

Before eighty four years we went to reside in Puranik's house in Red Jogeshwari Lane. It is generally supposed that man's memory becomes weak in old age and this supposition is true to a certain extent. I can lower an exception to this supposition. Even at the ripe age of ninety my memory is strong and I remember everything which I heard or saw from time to time when I was three or four years old.

This Puranik's house number was 85, Budhwar. There

was an *otha*—a sit-out outside the house but adjacent to the outer wall. There was a small Ganapati temple on this *otha* for construction of Laxmi Road a great portion of Puranik's house was acquired by Municipality of Pune city. But the image of Sri Ganapati was not removed from its original place which comes just in the centre of the road. A tiny temple was erected over this image and it remained there for some time. But Mr. S. G. Barve who was commissioner of Municipal Corporation thought that the temple was hindrance to the general traffic. He selected a place on the roadside nearby and built a temple. When the structure was complete he got the image of Ganapati removed from its original temple in the centre of the road and installed with due rites in the new temple. In this way the obstruction to the free traffic was removed. I had heard of transfers of government servants but not of Gods! But in this particular instance I came to know that human beings can also transfer Gods for their own convenience.

In widening the road a great portion of Puranik's house went under Laxmi road. There are only two shops in the vicinity of the road. They were newly built by Puranik and he receives rent thereof.

Puranik's family was originally resident of Nagarsul in Nasik District. Kaka's elder brother also recited Purana. It is not known when their family came to Pune. But from Kaka's talk there is reason to infer that Kaka and his elder brother must have come to Pune in about 1848 or thereabout.

At the age of 13 Kaka was having lessons from his brother in *rupavali* and *samaschakra*—Sanskrit grammer. Vasudev Shastri Parvalikar was his companion. Kaka's brother imparted instruction to them both. Both of them were staunch devotees of Sri Datta. They studied their lessons together and passed their spare time in the service of Sri Datta.

Once they entertained an idea to go to Kurgaddi—formerly known as Kuravapur—for serving the God Sri Datta there. This village is on the bank of Krishna river. Those that have read Sri Gurucharitra must be knowing that the first nine chapters thereof are devoted to describe the life of Sripaada Srivallabha who was considered to be the incarnation of Sri Datta. Kaka and his friend clandestinely absconded from their respective homes and went to Kurgaddi.

At this very time, Sri Narsimha Saraswati Swami who was spiritual Guru of Maharishi Annasaheb Patwardhan and who later on came to reside at Alandi, was lying down on the sandy bank of the Krishna. In the vicinity of this great Mahatma, Kaka and Vasudev Shastri were lying down on the sand for thirteen days. On the thirteenth day both of them had dreams. A Sanyasi told Kaka in his dream that he should recite Purana and to Vasudev Shastri he told that he should be a *nayyayik*—an authority on Sanskrit grammar. In older times people had great faith in God and therefore God was ever at their back. In this connection we are reminded of the well-known instance of Tukaram Maharaj who was lying on the bank of Indrayani river with intention to recover his *abhangs* which were thrown into the river by his rivals. He fasted during that period and offered his prayers by means of *Bhajan*. On the thirteenth day his *abhangs* appeared on the surface of the water of the Indrayani and his object was fulfilled.

These persons had full faith on the word of Sri Krishna that his devotee would never perish. Kaka and Vasudev Shastri were lying down on the bank of the Krishna river with a firm faith that God would never give them over.

Kaka and Vasudev Shastri then returned to Pune. Kaka was rather puzzled by a sort of dilemma before him. In his dream he was clearly told to recite Purana. But how could he do it without the knowledge of Sanskrit. He was therefore at a loss to find the way out. His companion Vasudev Shastri was also perplexed the same way. Both of them were, however, confident that what they heard in their dreams would never be false. Both of them, therefore, calmly waited to see what would happen in immediate future.

At that time there was a vacancy of a Puranik's post in 'Belbag' at Pune. The then manager of Belbag temple had a dream that the vacancy should be filled by appointing Bindu Madhav for reciting Purana before the God Sri Vishnu. The manager came to the house of Bindu Madhav. But when he saw that Kaka was then merely a boy of thirteen he was rather struck dumb. The manager thought that this boy would not be fit for the requisite post. So he came back without saying anything to Kaka. Night came on and the manager had the same dream that night. In fact, it was not an easy affair to recite Purana in Belbag. It was a *samsthan*—county of Nana Phadnis and its reputation was great. Those that recited Purana in that temple were learned men. To appoint a boy of thirteen on such a responsible post would merely be derision. On one hand the above thoughts were revolving in the manager's mind and on the other he could not but disobey a repeated direction in his dream. His mind was, so to speak, in a dilemmatic condition. He, however, made up his mind to try Bindu Madhav by giving him a chance.

The manager went to Bindu Madhav over again and invited him to recite Purana in Belbag in the afternoon of that day. Bindu Madhav alias Kaka accepted the invitation and in the afternoon went to Belbag. He occupied the raised seat on which the former Puraniks used to sit and recite Purana. He untied the *pothi*—scripture of Mahabharata which was already placed before his seat and began to recite Purana. Kaka then a boy of thirteen, recited Purana on that day for a couple of hours. The audience was wonder struck to see that the boy should have explained the passage from Mahabharata in a lucid manner and it was therefore spellbound. Audience present there felt that Saraswati the Goddess of learning was herself on the tongue of this boy when he was reciting Purana. The manager of Belbag stood speechless. All person expressed words of admiration about this boy and dispersed. From that time Kaka recited Purana in Belbag for 53 years till he was 66 years of age and conquered the minds of hearers throughout that long period.

Many times I happened to hear his Purana. As I was very young I did not know what were the best qualities of an orator; but I could even then know that Kaka's speech was quite unimpeded when he explained the incidents from any Purana and that he thereby made his audience stone-still.

I had heard about events from Kaka's boyish days. All this history I had actually heard from Kaka himself. I never thought that any of those events had any tinge of falsehood. I never doubted about his greatness.

Many students came to Kaka for learning Sanskrit and became expert in it. Kaka never charged any fee to them. Vasunana Charegaokar was one of his pupils. Vasunana was really a block-head; but Kaka loved him very much. Kaka tried his utmost to explain to him Sanskrit verse but he was not quick in grasping what he was taught. Kaka sometimes smiled in jest and said to Vasunana, 'You are indeed a hard stone.' But Kaka was ultimately successful to make him expert in Sanskrit. Vasunana became an expert Puranik and thereafter he recited Purana for number of years before Sri Ram in Tulsibag temple in Pune. As a Puranik he attained high fame.

Kaka never referred to any *pothi* or a holy book while teaching his students. Kaka's knowledge was the result of God's favour upon him. When a man has knowledge of omniscient God, he gets knowledge of everything. This principle was fully true in case of Kaka Puranik. Gulabrao Maharaj of Amravati was blind from his childhood, but he had vast knowledge of everything. If any one asked him any question he used to give him an answer immediately. Dnyaneshwar wrote his Dnyaneshwari, a gloss on Bhagwat-Gita, when he was fifteen years of age! Trust when Sri *Vishweshwar*—God Almighty favours any one, it is no wonder his favourite should have knowledge of what is in this universe. This was true in the case of Kaka whose vast knowledge of Sanskrit literature surprised even great scholars.

I remember that Prof. Dharap of the Fergusson College had been to Kaka, for getting a certain question solved. He asked Kaka whether a plot in a certain Sanskrit Drama had an authority in any Purana. Kaka at once told him that the story of the dram appeared in a particular chapter of a certain Purana and the author of the drama has deviated from it from some particulars for his suitable purpose. Kaka, without looking into the Purana, had forthwith given to Prof. Dharap.

I resided in the Kaka's *wada*—residence for nearly twelve years; but I never found him referring to any *pothi* before answering any question relating to any Purana. He had in his library Mahabharata, Ramayana, Bhagwat and other Sanskrit Puranas and other works of Sanskrit authors. The above *pothis* are at present with Bajirao Vishnu Puranik who is the grandson of Kaka's elder brother, Abajiboa.

I am causally reminded of Abajiboa. His life also was worthy of note. He was an expert Puranik. His voice was sweet and he was fond of singing. He used to recite Purana in the temple of Vithoba in Vithalwadi at Mumbai. It was only for four months every year. The remaining eight months he spent in Pune in practicing penance. He was all the while content with what he got. Owing to his contentment he was ever happy. In Pune, he annually got cloth and cash worth about three or four thousand rupees.

Once he was, with all the members of his family going to Kashi. There being no railway communication in those days all of them were travelling in bullock carts. They had taken with them two tents and necessary utensils. While travelling they were in a village in the Satpuda mountain. In the morning tents were raised. In one tent food was cooked and men were about to take their dinner. Just at that time a band of 40 or 50 *Bhillas*—tribal bandits—came and formed a circle round the tent. Such a raid was quite unexpected and frightful both. The females were struck with terror and were rooted to their spot. Abajiboa, was however, unmoved. He was calm and quiet. He having no greed for anything was naturally not frightened in any way.

He came out of his tent. He asked the raiders, 'who are you and what brings you here? What do you want from us?'

The leader of the *Bhillas* said that all of them had been there to commit robbery.

To this Abajiboa calmly said to the leader, "*Naik,* your plan I now perfectly understand. I have only to make you a request which I hope will be granted. All the persons—children and elderly persons are hungry. They are taking their meals. Kindly wait till we all take our food. When we finish our dinner you may take away all our belongings. If, however, you do not choose to wait till then you are at liberty to take away everything belonging to us even at this moment. We do not mind if all of us will have to be starved. We shall think that God wishes to starve us today."

"You may take your food, we shall wait till then." The *naik* said.

Abajiboa entered the tent. He saw that women were burring their ornaments. He told them that they should not burry even a single ornament. "I have promised to handover all our things to the band of *Bhillas*." Abajiboa said. "We shall therefore take our food and handover all our things to them."

All the persons finished their dinner and came out of

the tent. Abajiboa then handed over everything to the *Bhillas*. He did not keep anything behind.

The women voluntarily handed their ornaments to the *Bhillas*.

The *Bhillas* took all the things and departed. As soon as the *Bhillas* walked over a small distance Abajiboa ran after them. The *naik* of the Bhillas stopped at the call of Abajiboa. The latter said to the *naik* that he forgot to hand over his diamond ring and gave it to him. The *naik* said that he had not seen that precious ring and in these circumstances why he was handing it over to him.

Abajiboa said, "You had a mind to take all our belongings. This ring remained to be given to you through oversight. So I have come to hand it over to you."

Without saying anything further the *naik* took the ring and went away along with other *Bhillas*.

The persons in Abajiboa's camp asked him, "The *Bhillas* have taken away all the things required in our travelling. What next?"

Abajiboa replied, "Why are you anxious about it? The God who took our care uptil now will not fail to do it in future. Wait and see what happens."

In the afternoon three or four *Bhillas* came to Abajiboa. They had brought with them rice pulse, wheat flour, ghee, sugar etc and gave all the articles to Abajiboa. The *Bhillas* said that their *naik* has sent these articles for their evening meals. Cooking utensils followed suit.

Thereafter the *naik* himself visited Abajiboa and asked him as to where they came and where they were going.

Abajiboa said, "We reside in Pune and are going to Kashi on pilgrimage. My occupation is to recite Purana."

The *naik* then questioned, "Will you please recite Purana this night?"

Abajiboa told him that he would do so provided he returned his *pothi*.

The *naik* agreed with this. The *Bhillas* swept the open space clean and then they went away.

After sometime a *Bhilla* brought the requisite *pothi* and at night, nearly four or five hundred *Bhillas* came to hear the Purana. Abajiboa took the story of Ekalavya *Bhilla* as a subject matter of his Purana. The *Bhillas* were extremely pleased when they knew the history of Ekalavya from Abajiboa. After the end of Purana the *naik* said that the Purana should continue for four or five days more. Abajiboa conceded, and his Purana continued for the stated period.

On the last day the *Bhillas* made a great festival in honour of Abajiboa. They returned all the articles which they had carried away from his tent and offered him three excellent idols of Ram, Sita and Laxman. In addition they gave him one thousand and one rupees. They also gave two *Bhillas* with him for protection in the course of his journey.

The three idols received by Abajiboa are present at Chinchwad in his grand-son's house.

I heard this charming account from Kaka. It was really an amusement to hear it. On hearing that account a thought was then uppermost in my mind that God gives help to those who are free from greed and selfishness. Sri Krishna has given a promise to his devotees that the responsibility of protecting them lies on him. His promise never comes to be untrue. In those times I had put my faith in the words of Lord Sri Krishna, and that faith has not impaired in the least in my ripe old age.

Kaka had ever been a devotee of Sri Datta from the time he returned from Kurgaddi at the age of thirteen. He called himself as a disciple of Baba Vaikar. I am going to give the history of Baba in the next chapter of this book. I do not know the occasion when Kaka and Baba met together. I also do not know when Baba had an opportunity to admit Kaka in the folds of his disciples. When Kaka told something about his Guru Baba, the latter was not living.

Barring the time spent in reciting Purana in Belbag, Kaka spent all the time in meditation. Kaka from time to time used to say, 'अतिसारेण मरणं योगिनामपि दुर्लभम्.'

In the end Kaka also suffered from diarrhoea. He told his son that he would not survive that illness and that his end was near. While getting up from the bed his head dashed on a pillar nearby. At that time he remarked, "Now it is a question of eight days, how many times will you dash against my head?" This was addressed to the pillar.

The milk woman Gangabai came and asked Kaka for money for satisfying the bill of milk. "How long will you ask money from me?" To her he said, "You should, from hence, take it from my son Nanba."

Nanba was now capable of managing the family affairs.

Kaka's illness prevented him from going to Belbag for Purana. This was after fifty three years service as Puranik. One Ganoba Kelkar had been present to hear his Purana from the beginning to end. He came to Kaka and asked him, "Are you well prepared for your end?"

Kaka said to him, "Ganoba, it is strange that you who heard my Purana for fifty three years should ask me such a question. Do you think that a man like me who explained to you the principles of Vedanta in the course of my Purana should have been neglectful of those principles and the practice thereof?"

Kaka had been uttering the name *Datta Avadhut*. A week had elapsed since he became ill. His end was coming near and near. He had previously declared the day on which he will pass away. On the stated day the Sun came to the Meriden at 12 noon. He was perfectly conscious. In that state he uttered the name of *Datta Avadhut* and closed his eyes for gong. He passed away, leaving his flame behind.

As I was a boy I did not attend his funeral procession but elder brother attended it. I came to know that many learned men were present at Omkareshwar where his body was to be cremated. Among them was his lifelong companion Vasudev Shastri Parvatikar. This was the person who had gone to Kurgaddi with Kaka and lying on the sandy bank of the Krishna river for thirteen days along with him. Both of them had realized the dreams they had while so lying there. Kaka became a Puranik and Vasudev Shastri became a famous *nayyayik*.

When Kaka's dead body was placed on funeral pier Vasudev Shastri overpowered by sorrow said, "Oh Madhavji, you are going ahead of me leaving me behind in grief, but I too will follow you exactly after six months."

And it is really wonderful that this Vasudev Shastri left this world exactly after six months to see his companion in the next world!

Baba Vaikar

I was really surprised when Kaka Puranik narrated miracles of some saints. While listening to them I never thought that he was telling me anything but truth. Man's boyhood is a proper period to know the stories of saint's occult powers. They create sort of belief about them, and tend to enlarge and give a permanent place in his mind. When a man is young he is ever prone to disbelieve stories about the exercise of occult powers. Youths generally rely upon their eyes, to believe in matters they see. They are therefore slow to believe in matters unseen by them. It was not so with me.

From the time I was nearly five years old I had company of saintly persons off and on. I shunned the company of persons who were non-believers of God. I readily believed in matters which were being told about the miracles which saints worked in their life time.

Bindu Madhav alias Kaka Puranik sometimes referred to strange incidents in the life of one Baba Vaikar. Kaka considered him as his Guru. Kaka was therefore an authority to narrate the miraculous incidents from Baba's life. Kaka had not the least cause to tell lies or exaggerate matters in any way. Although I was unable to explain the causes and effects of those incidents owing to my tender age, I am now enabled, in the evening of my life explain away those miracles, as my thoughts have been perfectly settled owing to a long experience.

I was fifteen years of age when I heard from Kaka Puranik about several amazing events from the life of Baba Vaikar. I am narrating them here under.

The place of residence of Baba's ancestors is unknown. I do not remember if Kaka ever told me about it. Baba Vaikar was unmarried. He was therefore free from the cares of a householder. Baba's father had been a firm devotee of God. Baba also worshipped Sri Datta. Baba's father once had no money to celebrate the *navaratra*—nine nights festival. He was therefore uneasy. He said to his wife that the annual festival of *navaratra* would have to be dropped as he had no money for that purpose.

In those times everything was very cheap. Five rupees were more than sufficient for celebrating the *navaratra*. A day before the commencement of the *navaratra*, Baba had gone to his field. In his absence a gentleman on horse back came to his residence. Seeing that Baba's father was not at home he handed over five rupees to his wife saying, "Tell your husband that he should not postpone *navaratra* for want of money. Tell him also that one Martandrao has given five rupees for celebrating the festival."

When Baba's father returned from his field his wife handed over five rupees to him saying that one Martandrao visited his house during his absence and had given the amount for Navaratra. He was on horseback, the horse being white.

Hearing the name of Martandrao tears rose in the eyes of Baba's father. He at once understood that the rider on white horse was none but the presiding deity of the Navaratra. He was grieved to see that he was extremely unfortunate that though the God Khandoba came to his house he could not see him.

Then he told his wife that Martandrao was the God Malhari Martand, and that they had to celebrate His Navaratra. As He Himself had supplied the requisite amount, Navaratra ought to be celebrated with all due rites. Accordingly it was celebrated with all joy.

Saint Namdev was similarly in monetary difficulties and Sri Vithal of Pandharpur had in the name of Keshav Sheti furnished his home with all supplies. From these instances it is evident that God always runs to rescue His devotees when He sees them in difficulties. I know several such instances but our limits forbid us to describe them. However I have firm faith in the principle above referred to. Great saint Shri Tukaram Maharaj in his *abhang* has said the same thing. He says, 'पडता जड भारी। दासीं आठवावा हरी।। मग तो होऊ नेदी शीण। आड घाली सुदर्शन।। हरिनामाच्या चिंतनें। पळती बारा वाटा विघ्नें।।'

I had never the boldness to say that the principle laid down in this above *abhanga* by Tukaram is false. Logical discussion in these matters falls short of explaining this divine power. There is therefore no other way than implicitly believing such matters, as they are almost beyond the intellectual grasp of human beings.

Being unmarried Baba was free from all cares. His daily programme was to wander on pilgrimage to holy places. He was always accompanied by his two disciples viz. Pandharinath and Ayyaramboa. They begged alms wherever they went and cooked food for them all. Baba spent his morning time in worshipping Sri Datta, and meditation. In the evening Baba used to recite Datta kavacha and *Bhajan*. On this occasion a wooden seat was placed before Baba. Kaka Puranik told us that the God Sri Datta was actually sitting on the wooden seat at the time of Baba's *Bhajan*. This was due to Baba's earnest worship to that God. I was really astonished to hear it form Kaka. I, in fact knew then that the idol of stone Pandurang of Pandharpur, was actually eating the food offered to it by Namdeo. God has other way of favouring a person firmly devoted to him but I could not then believe that God would appear before his worshipper in a bodily form. But now I have got its explanation in the Yoga-sutra: '*स्वाध्यायादिष्ट देवता संप्रयोग: ।*'

Swadhyaya includes muttering of a mantra relating to any God. When the mantra is muttered for a stated number o times God appears before his devotee actually in bodily form, or appears before him in his dream or gives him his own power. Baba had been serving Sri Datta without break for several years. There was therefore no wonder if Sri Datta daily paid him a visit. When a man's devotion reaches its highest pitch God is actually visible to him. This principle is now ever occupying my mind.

Baba possessed some divine powers. Once he had gone to Ambajogai. He had his stay there in a *dharmashalla*—a charitable rest house for travellers. The then *tahasildar*—a collector—there had misappropriated Nizam Governments money. Government therefore had sent some Arabs to arrest him. As soon as the tahasildar got scent of this he ran away from his house and straightway went to the *dharmashalla*. He fell at Baba's feet and earnestly requested him to save him from that calamity. Baba asked him not to be afraid. He asked him to sit near him to avoid arrest. He assured the tahasildar that as long as he was sitting by his side the Arabs would not see him.

The Arabs, on inquiry came to know that the tahasildar had entered the *dharmashalla*. Though he was sitting near Baba, the Arabs could not see him. By means of his divine power Baba had made the tahasildar invisible.

When the Arabs took their departure from *dharmashalla*, Baba permitted the tahasildar to go home. The tahasildar said to Baba that he would never forget his obligations. He requested Baba to pay a visit to his house. Baba told him that he never visited any one's house and that he should not therefore press him to do it. He further said, "You need not be in any way anxious, none will arrest you now."

The tahasildar again fell at Baba's feet and went home without any anxiety. It is the saint's nature to offer protection to those who seek it from them.

While on pilgrimage Baba with his associates was in a thick jungle on his way to Sri Shailya. While travelling in that jungle he lost his way and travelled a long distance in the wrong direction. Being fatigued he had no other way than to stop in the midst of that thick jungle. The sky kissing trees and the wild creepers inter woven with one another served as a night resort to the beasts of pray created awe-inspiring sensation in the mind of those who accompanied Baba. Baba was, however very calm and quiet. He also told his disciples to calmly wait and see what would happen in a short time. He said that God would send some one as a guide to take us to the right path. Sometime passed and they heard the noise of an eagle's wings. That creature, while flying minimized its speed just over the place where Baba and others were sitting. Baba got up and so also others. The eagle's wings had cast a big shadow on the ground. Baba and his disciples were following that shadow. In a very short time they came to the right path. They found that they had not strayed long.

When the eagle came flying with a great noise over their head Baba told his disciples that God had sent the bird as their guide. They were conveyed by its shadow to the proper path. Baba told his disciples to make a bow to the eagle. Baba and others bowed to the eagle and the creature which had slowed down its speed, enhanced it in a great measure and disappeared in the sky in a short time. Baba and his disciples soon went at the foot of the mountain, on which the temple of God Shiva was situated. There are a number of steps in that mountain which a traveller has to ascend before he reaches the temple.

As soon as Baba reached near the flight of steps at the foot of the mountain he saw a gigantic bull sitting on the first flight facing Baba. The bull was nearly ten feet tall. It was an uncommon and surprising phenomenon. They thought that such a gigantic bull was impossibility on earth. Baba therefore inferred that it must be the divine bull-conveyance of Shiva. He conjectured that God Shiva was present there in the form of his conveyance.

Baba and others bowed to the big animal and without taking the trouble of approaching the temple resumed their journey.

While on pilgrimage Baba went to Gangapur. During the period of his stay there one Kau Akka went to see him. This lady, by great penance, had attained high position as a saint. She was born in rich family and also married to one who was also very rich. But when she was sixteen years of age her husband died. This hard stroke of destiny freed her mind from worldly affection and passions. All the while she was absorbed in meditation, as she could not find any charm in worldly affections. She therefore made up her mind to go to Gangapur and pass her barren life in the service of God. The family of her birth and the family in which she was married were rich. Members of both these families tried much to change her mind and give up the idea of going to Gangapur but in vain. Her resolve was firm.

She went to Gangapur. She daily begged alms in dressed food and spent her entire time in practicing penance.

When she met Baba Vaikar she told him her own history and expressed her desire to accompany him on pilgrimage. Baba said "You are yet very young, we go to holy places on foot and you will not be able to walk with us. Besides some time we get to eat, sometimes not. In these circumstances it will be very difficult for you to join our company. We have no objection if you come with us but you will have to undergo privation. Think about this and then come to a decision."

"Baba," Kau Akka said, "I have thought over these matters when the calamity of my husband's premature death freed me from the shackles of worldly life and drove me to lead my present life of solitude. I have surrendered my remaining life to the service of God. I take you to be my father; so considering that I am your own daughter, I earnestly request you to take me with you."

Considering her firm resolves Baba could not slight her request, and her proposal was accepted. Baba then called his disciples and told them, "consider Kau Akaka as your sister and give her every help and protection in our pilgrimage." Baba's word was law to them.

Baba left Gangapur with his disciples and Kau Akka and resumed their journey. On their way the disciples begged alms, Kau Akka cooked and all used to take their food. This programme was going on for a number of years. One day Baba said to Kau Akka and others that he was ordered by Sri Data Maharaj to go to Kashi. Accordingly they all went to Kashi. From times immemorial it has been the conviction of all Hindus that a man dying in Kashi gets salvation. It is said that Sri Vishveshwar recites a certain mantra at the time of man's death, and it frees him from taking births in future.

At Kashi Baba's conversation with Kau Akka and his disciples gave reason for them to infer that Baba's end was nearer. One day Baba clearly told them all that he would pass away very soon. He said to his disciples that after his obsequious were over they should convey Kau Akka to Gangapur, and then should go on visiting holy places as before.

Kau Akka, by this time was very much advanced in age. To her Baba said that she should go to Gangapur, serve Sri Data Maharaj there and guide the pilgrims according to his advice. He further said, "you are now in favour of Sri Data Maharaj. He will therefore honour your word and therefore your word will be true."

After a few days Baba called Kau Akka, Pandharinath and Ayyaramboa near him and said to them that he was passing away for good in a short time. So saying he put his head on the lap of his disciple Ayyaramboa and surrendered his last breath to Heaven.

Pandharinath felt anxiety for his Guru's funeral as none had money to spend for it. At this time they heard a sound of something burst. They saw a hole at the top of Baba's head and a stream of pure whitish water running out of it.

Ayyaramboa asked Pandharinath if he knew Baba's command. The latter questioned him as to what it was. Ayyaramboa said that it was unnecessary to cremate Baba's dead body, as water of Ganges is issuing from his head. It is a hint to us that the body should be offered to the river Ganges. Accordingly they left Baba's body in the river Ganges and all of them were free from anxiety. Both the disciples had to carry out the injunctions of their revered Guru.

Both of them were unmarried. They had no ties. They were their own masters to go anywhere they liked. They brought Kau Akka to Gangapur and then they again resumed their pilgrimage.

As directed by Baba, Kau Akka remained at Gangapur till the close of her life. Throughout her life she went on giving advice to the pilgrims who visited that holy place. The pilgrims had actually dreams to effect that they should go to Kau Akka and act upto her direction and that their difficulties would be removed. Herself she had nothing to accomplish but spent her whole life in advising the needy in matters divine. She was greatly revered by all in Gangapur. She lived on alms. The worshippers of Sri Data managed to convey cooked food to her at noon time. She never went out for it. She never accepted anything from anyone. She had the power of reading the minds of those who went to her for putting their grievances before her and asking for remedy to redress them. At such a time she knew what was passing in their minds and before they asked any question she used to answer it. She had also foresight of future events. She thus put men on their guard against forthcoming dangers.

In this regard my own brother had experience about her knowledge of future events. My elder brother Mr. Gangadhar graduated in 1891. His nickname was Tatyasaheb. He was very pious man. English education had not in any way affected his religious opinions. After passing B.A. he intended to go to Gangapur and recite *Gurucharitra* in three days. He apprized Kaka Puranik of his intention. Kaka advised him to put up at Kau Akka's place of residence and carry out his plan under her guidance.

My brother went to Gangapur and saw Kau Akka there. He said that Kaka Puranik had asked him to put up at yours. Kau Akka said, "Alright, stay with me as long as you are here." Tatyasaheb then expressed his desire to finish reading *Gurucharitra* within three days to which Kau

Akka replied, "Tatya, do you think that reading *Gurucharitra* is tantamount to mowing grass in the field? If you want to read it you must do it with all attention. Thereby you fully grasp the events in the lives of Sripad Sri Vallabha and Sri Narsimha Saraswati, and leaves a lasting effect of their lives on your mind. It strengthens your faith about God and you never swerve from righteous path. God is graceful to such a man. When once you are engaged in the management of your household affairs you will hardly get time to visit this holy place over again. You therefore, stay here for a week and finish the reading of *Gurucharitra* within seven days. Your daily reading must be complete before midday. After your reading is over you should go to a particular person for bringing a bread from him. I get sufficient food to feed even three or four persons. But it is a rule here that a pilgrim should give up his dignity and beg alms, and I tell you to bring a bread; otherwise I can supply you with sufficient food. You should, after you take your food, go on muttering the name of God whom you like. In the evening you should go for *arti*—devotional singing—in the temple. God is great, and he will always show his favour to you.'

My brother had his stay in the room of Kau Akka. He arranged his programme according to Kau Akka's advice. In the morning he read Gurucharitra. Then he brought a bread of *madhukari* and dined with Kau Akka. In the evening he used to go out for a walk.

On the fifth day Kau Akka said to my brother that he should not go out for a walk in the evening. When my brother asked her the reason why he should not go out she only replied, "You will come to know it in the evening."

After dinner my brother had been sitting with Kau Akka in her residence. Time was passing on. In the evening a raid of nearly 150 persons came to loot the house of *Pujari*—an appointed Brahmin worshiper in a temple. They came firing their guns and flourishing their swords. All the villagers ran to their homes and got their doors chained from within. There was not a single soul outside in the streets.

One of the dacoits' was scaling the wall of the *pujari* whose house they wanted to raid. *Pujari's* servant saw him scaling the wall. He pushed a big wooden beam in the direction of the wall where the dacoit was coming up and let it fall down. The bone of his thigh was fractured and he fell down in a pit nearly waist-deep. The pit was over flowing with dirty water. The dacoit was fully drenched in that water, in wounded condition. Some dacoits ran to his help, took him out from the ditch. They washed his body with clean water and dried it. As he could not walk four bearers conveyed him in *khadi* cloth. The gang of dacoits thought that the fall of one of them in a ditch of filthy water was an ill-omen and therefore all of them left the village with shouts of 'Din. . .Din.'

When they went away everywhere there was calm and quiet. After half an hour men came out of their resorts and there was traffic in the streets as usual.

Kau Akka said to my brother, "Now you must have known the reason why I prevented you from going out in the evening. Always keep in mind there is always your safety in abiding by the advice of elderly persons."

My brother was convinced that Kau Akka had the power of knowing what would take place in future and this power she had acquired by her life long penance and devotion. Deprived though she was of the comforts of married life owing to the premature demise of her husband, she served the human world and helped men to make their lives happy. Those that came in contact with her were freed from their difficulties. Though widowed in her prime of youth she never left courage. She never cared to enjoy her life on the strength of riches of her father or her deceased husband. She took lessons of *vairagya*—absence of worldly desire or passion—from her Guru and came to Gangapur to spend the rest of her life in that holy place.

I do not know when Kau Akka ended her earthly career. I have given the foregoing account which Kaka Puranik told me from time to time. I have neither added nor subtracted anything from it.

50 *Saints Known to me*

Sarange Sanyasi

Suppose you see a boy singing like an expert and giving beautiful explanation of passages from Sanskrit literature without having received instructions in the art of singing or in Sanskrit language at any time before; would it not be a miracle evoking your admiration and surprise?

I personally know the life of such a person, whose name in latter portion of his life was Sarange Sanyasi.

When he was a boy of twelve, he was learning in vernacular 2nd standard in a primary school at Wai. He had encountered two previous failures in that standard and he appeared for the examination for the third time.

The day, on which his result was to be out, arrived. Clever boys were confident of their success; others were in a state of suspense. At about noon the result was at last out. The boy, who had failed twice before, again failed.

This was his third failure. With heavy steps he came home when the mid-day sun was awfully hot and unbearable. His body had copiously perspired, so much so that his shirt had been quite wet.

His heart was beating at the thought that he had soon to face his angry father. It was indeed a hard trial for him.

When his father saw him, he asked him about the result. At this question his body began to tremble with fright; and with his face downwards through shame, he replied in low tone, "I got plucked."

At this the father got enraged. In a fit of anger, he gave two or three blows to the son and drove him out of his house saying, "You failed thrice in second standard! You are a block-head! You get out; do not show me your face over again. Go on begging from door to door for your food. I have no sympathies for you."

The unfortunate boy stepped out of his house and stood stand-still, in the street under the scorching sun. "Where to go?" was a question before him in his homeless condition. Deprived of his parent's support, he said to himself, *'who will now give me food and shelter?'* He thought over it and at last an idea occurred to his mind that he should go to the Math of Gopalboa who was a great Saint at Wai.

The forlorn boy accordingly went crying to Gopalboa who asked him why he was crying. The boy told him all that had happened. Gopalboa was moved by what the boy told him. He called one of his disciples and directed him to take the boy with him. He said, "Let the boy first take his bath and food and then let him come to me." The boy after taking food came to Gopalboa.

After nearly half an hour, Gopalboa asked his disciples to give invitation to all the citizens to attend the Boy's *kirtan*—presenting cultural and theological stories along with holy songs—on the bank of the river Krishna.

As the invitation was from the Saint, vast multitude of persons came to hear the *kirtan*.

At 8 P.M. Gopalboa took the boy to the appointed place. The boy only mechanically accompanied Gopalboa to that place. He did not know why he was taken there. He did not know why so many persons had assembled there. He was merely a passive observer of what was passing before him.

Gopalboa then said to the boy, "Boa, these persons have gathered here to hear your *kirtan*... Now stand and begin..."

With these words he asked the boy to open his mouth. The boy opened his mouth and Gopalboa put a pinch of *vibhuti*— holy ashes on his tongue. The boy got up and at once began to sing initial prayer to God and sweet harmony was created by the musical instruments which were playing just in tune with the boy's voice. When the first song was over the boy took up a certain theological topic and he went on explaining it to the audience giving appropriate illustrations from Sanskrit literature. Then he chose a story from the Sanskrit epic to illustrate that topic. While narrating the story he sang at intervals poems in connection with that story. So he gave this performance for full three hours. His unimpeded oration together with comic cuts and masterly music kept the audience quite spell-bound. The *kirtan* was both interesting and instructive. Interest went on waxing from start to finish.

Those who heard it spoke highly of the boy's knowledge of Sanskrit and music. But the people at the same time wondered as to how the boy could have given this beautiful performance without the previous knowledge of either Sanskrit or music.

The boy's parents were among the audience. When they heard their son's *kirtan* they were greatly astonished. His father repented for having beaten him and driven him out of his house. They were at a loss to understand how their son who was a dunce in the morning came to display his knowledge in music and philosophy in his *kirtan* at night. His brain reeled. He was doubtful whether he was in a dream. He was confused. His reason could not work. Oh! A block-head who could not satisfy his examiners and abominably failed continuously for 3 years in second standard exhibiting great knowledge in music and philosophy in about eight hours after his failure! He found no explanation for it.

The audience dispersed after the *kirtan* was over. So also the Boy's parents went home with feelings of joy and sorrow both. They were delighted to see their son's wisdom and sorry for driving him out of their house.

Their sleepless night passed in brooding over the problem viz. the phenomenal change in their foolish son.

In the morning his parents went to Gopalboa and requested him to send their son with them. The latter said to them, "Now do not count him as your son. He will now make *kirtans* and see holy places. His fame as a *kirtankaar* will spread far and wide throughout the country."

At this the parents were disappointed and came home in a dejected mood.

Being directed by Gopalboa the boy took his leave, and followed the life of *kirtankaar*. His *kirtans* were so much liked and appreciated by the learned that everywhere they showered praises on him, and thus Gopalboa's prediction came to be true. People were astonished to find the boy exhibiting his deep knowledge in Vedanta philosophy. His singing charmed the people, and he had all this acquisition without study or practice at anytime before in his present life. Wherever he went he was admired and respected by all. His pet instrument was Sarangi—a stringed instrument like fiddle. His dexterous hand would play on it in such a manner that even the experts in that branch recognized his unique talent.

From the time he was twelve till he was twenty he visited many holy places. He had all the while been making *kirtans*. In the course of his journey he went to Akkalkot. At that time there was a very great Saint in that town. People worshipped him like God. Sarange Sanyasi paid homage to this saint, who asked him to go to Krishnananda to Kashi. Krishnananda was a Yogi endowed with divine powers. Accordingly he went to Krishnananda.

Krishnananda forthwith asked him, "Could not the saint of Akkalkot have given you Sanyas? Why did he send you here? Alright, all the formalities required for giving you Sanyas—order renunciating the worldly life—will be observed tomorrow." Thus the boy entered that order the next day. Krishnananda then advised him to go on pilgrimage.

From this time he wandered garbed in the robe of Sanyasi visiting the holy places. Since then he ceased to follow his profession as a *kirtankaar*.

At that time he used to see my father in Pune every year. Some days he was our guest till he had his stay at Pune. He was about 5 feet 9 inches tall. With white complexion, straight nose, sparkling eyes and lustrous face, his figure was most imposing. His pleasing personality was most attractive. He was always cheerful. I was ten when he paid first visit to our residence. I am now past eighty-five, but yet memory of that personage is not in the least obliterated from my mind. It yet stands before my mental eye with its particulars. Sarange Sanyasi and my father were always talking about theological matters in which they took equal interest. Sometimes hours after hours passed but their talk never ended. Though it was not my age to grasp and understand the subject of their conversation still a sort of reverence about Sarange Sanyasi was engendered in my mind; and it has not yet abated in the least.

When he was making *kirtans,* he had made friends with excellent singers and players on various musical instruments. These persons had the highest respect for Sarange Sanyasi as he had acquired mastery over singing and playing on musical instrument at such young age.

Once my father's cousin had been to see us in Pune. He was Police Sub Inspector. My father was customs officer to the Pune Police Superintendent. Sarange Sanyasi was then our guest. My father's cousin and my father were fond of hearing music. The cousin said to my father, "Baba, you are acquainted with Mishraji, a very renowned singer in India, so let me hear her singing."

My father requested Sarange Sanyasi to play on Sarangi as an accompaniment to Mishraji's singing. The Sanyasi said with a smile, "Babasaheb, would it now become me to attend a songstress' abode especially when I have renounced the world and am wearing a robe in token there of? But as I must honour your word I cannot refuse your call in order to avoid your displeasure."

At night my father, his cousin and Sarange Sanyasi went to Mishraji's house. My father and Sarange Sanyasi were acquainted with Mishraji. Seeing the Sanyasi she was greatly delighted. She gave her valuable shawl for his seat. Being apprised of their purpose to go to her, she at once took the stringed instrument viz. Sarangi and gave it to Sarange Sanyasi. She began to sing and the Sanyasi began to play on the Sarangi as an accompaniment of her singing. The performance was grand and it lasted for full three hours. It was a sumptuous feast to the ears. Then all left her residential quarters and came home. My father's cousin thought himself to be extremely fortunate to have had the precious opportunity of hearing Mishraji. The Sanyasi and Mishraji were both experts in their arts and they fully appreciated each other's merit.

For several days hereafter I was hearing the description of this programme, given by my father. I am also fond of hearing music but I being then a young boy I was not taken to Mishraji's house. I had to remain satisfied only with the description given by my father; but when I subsequently took lessons in singing I began to feel for having missed the valuable opportunity of hearing Mishraji's song and Sarange Sanyasi's Sarangi. It is a common place experience that man loses many such momentous occasions for one reason or another; and howsoever he feels sorry for it for the opportunity once lost never returns.

Then Sarange Sanyasi left our house and went on pilgrimage. Exactly a year after, he came to us again. This was his third visit to our house. By this time he must be twenty three. For a couple of days he had his stay at ours. On the second day he abruptly said to my father, "Babasaheb, this visit of mine may perhaps prove to be the last one, for it seems that the Almighty wills that way."

I remember his words. But in those tender years of mine the idea of death was far away from me. I did not definitely know that someday a man is required to die. Men sometimes talk about such matters in vague terms the meaning whereof cannot be deciphered by small boys.

Sarange Sanyasi took his leave and again resumed his wandering.

After five or six months sad news of his death fell on our ears. My father shed tears. We also were grieved and shed tears. The picture of my father shedding tears on hearing the news of Sarange Sanyasi's death is yet before my eyes.

That Sarange Sanyasi who was a dunce in his boyish days had a sudden change in his life owing to Gopalboa's favour is indeed a miracle in the eyes of laymen. But we find explanation of such miracles in Vedanta and Yoga philosophies.

Man has had innumerable previous births. All his actions whether good or bad and all his desires are stored in mind in atomic form. When a man dies the individual soul leaves the earthly body and takes the mind and five other senses with him. With this material he enters another body and his new life begins. The impressions imbibed on the mind in previous birth are not totally effaced but they are dormant. Owing to peculiar circumstances such impressions are awakened.

Sarange Sanyasi must therefore have studied music and theology in his former life, memory thereof was revised by his contact with the saint Gopalboa and he at once stood before the world as the best *kirtankaar*.

60   *Saints Known to me*

Hariboa of Phaltan

*T*his great saint has conferred immense obligations on our family.

To him the entire universe was his home. Never did he wear any clothes nor did he ever care for his food; but he devoted his life in caring for clothing and feeding others. Like a wandering bird he was not confined to any particular place. Now he was here, now there and sometimes nowhere. Like the Almighty God he was all pervading. Like God his origin could not be traced. His birth and parentage, his antecedents and associations were all *en* shrouded in mystery which was never solved. He was conversant with Marathi, Telugu and Malayalam languages. When he chanted his prayers in one of these languages he was beside himself with joy. Those who listened to his chanting were so much absorbed in it that they were also delighted and entranced.

Some eighty five years back my father was a clerk in the Police office at Indapur of Pune District. Here he came in close contact with this great saint. His association continued for the period of three years. Several miracles which this mystic saint performed during this period were narrated to me by my father. They were then noted down by me.

When my father chanced to have a contact with this saint, India was ruled by the British. There was plenty of everything. Income of Rs.4 was enough to maintain the family of four or five members. The salary of the headmaster of a primary school was Rs.4 per month, that of a clerk Rs.7 per month. My father was appointed clerk on Rs.7 per month though he had never applied for that post. Within eight months he got promotion of Re. 1. My father being intelligent and ambitious he could not find any charm in service, with such a meagre salary. He was sure that he could get much more elsewhere in any other field. So he thought of leaving the service. Soon after this thought crossed his mind he happened to meet the saint. He at once questioned my father "Why do you think of leaving your present service?"

"Who told you so?" asked father.

"Am I required to be told?" Hariboa countered with smile.

My father replied that his present income was insufficient to meet his expenses and hence he thought so.

The saint asked, "How much do you want?"

In those days revenue clerk who put in 25 years' service used to get maximum pay of Rs.25/- before retirement.

My father told Hariboa that he would be satisfied if he would get Rs.30/- per month.

"Alright," Hariboa said, "I would give you that much monthly salary on the 19th day from today. But give up the idea of resigning."

And strange to say that exactly on the 19th day, that my father received an order of the police superintendent to see him in his camp. My father accordingly saw him. The superintendent asked him to take charge of deputy customs officer post in his office. When the superintendent got satisfied with his work he confirmed my father on that post on Rs.30/-per month and extra Rs.15 per month as permanent travelling allowance. My father thus superseded nearly six hundred servants above him and got the post, which but for the saint's Godly assurance was quite an impossibility.

This sudden and unexpected uplift in pecuniary condition resulted in placing our family in comfortable position. My father got then the right to appear for an examination for Magistrate's post in which he came out successful.

He exercised magisterial powers for sixteen years and then he retired from government service. Under those circumstances, he could give us, both brothers, college education. Both of us became pleaders and prospered in our profession. We could also afford to give higher education to our sons. In this way Hariboa's favour brought our family in the fore. Hariboa had completely renounced the world. He therefore never cared for any garment to cover his body. He was nude. Sky was his covering and bare ground his comfortable bed. His body was so to speak immune from scorching heat of summer, severe cold of winter and torrential rains of monsoons. Every season was the same to this nude saint. To show favour to any one or to withhold it was in fact his whim. My father had great respect for him. It may be some of the reasons why the saint looked after my father's interest. It is true however their hearts were firmly united.

One day my father had to go out for some business early in the morning. While passing by the street he saw at some distance something shining in the slanting rays of the morning sun. When he came in its vicinity he found that it was an image of God Hanuman embossed on a silver sheet. My father looked around. No one was present nearby. He took the sheet up and put it into his pocket. At about 10 in the morning he was passing by a shop in the bazaar. Hariboa was sitting in this shop. He called my father by his name. My father entered the shop in response to his call. Hariboa in his joyful mood asked my father as to what was in his pocket. My father had almost forgotten that he had found an image of God Hanuman early in the morning. He therefore told Hariboa that there was nothing in his pocket. At this Hariboa said, "Why do you hide it from me?"

Hariboa then gave description of the image and asked my father to take it out. My father took it out and handed it over to him. Hariboa thereupon placed it on his head, then on his shoulders and danced in ecstasy. He then returned the image to my father saying, "Today is Saturday sacred to the deity. It is considered to be the day of God Hanuman. Have a fast today and keep on fasting on every Saturday hereafter. God will bless you and look after your welfare."

My father in obedience to this advice kept on fasting on Saturdays for nearly forty years till his death; and according to the word of Hariboa, my father's life was a grand success. Hariboa never went to any one for taking his food. But when he first told my father to fast on Saturdays, Hariboa took his food at my father's, the same evening. All thought that it was an exceptional favour shown to my father by Hariboa.

There was at that time a gentleman named Narsingrao Deshpande living at Indapur. He was a firm devotee of Hariboa. Every day he used to see the saint and then took his food. He fasted on the day if he could not find out the saint.

Narsingrao had once an attack of typhoid. Fever continued for 42 days. He was in delirious condition. He used to remember Hariboa off and on. On the 42nd day Hariboa tapped the outer door of his house. The door was opened. Hariboa entered the house and straightway went to the patient to whom he said, "Why were you calling me so long?"

So saying Hariboa sat on the emaciated body of Narsingrao, caught hold of his hands and with a sudden shocking jerk made him sit. All the relatives of the patient thought that the patient must have succumbed to this harsh treatment but to the surprise of them all; the patient opened his eyes and said that he was very hungry.

Hariboa said, "The fever is gone, he will not die. Give him a little rice and let him sleep. From tomorrow he will be alright." Narsingrao had a sound sleep. When he awoke the next morning he was completely free from fever and in a few days he fully recovered.

I am now giving you another incident which will testify to Hariboa's great powers as a Yogi. There was a merchant at Indapur. His name was Vishnudas Naagar. He was always pressing Hariboa to show him some miracle.

Hariboa said to him, "Why do you want miracles? Of what use are they to you? You better take to your trade and make money." With all this, Vishnudas was not satisfied. He persisted in his usual request.

On a certain day Hariboa went in front of the house of Vishnudas and called him out at midnight hour. It was a dark night. Vishnudas came out in response to the call. Hariboa asked him to put on his dress and accompany him. He said that he was going to show him some miracle. Vishnudas accompanied him to a field outside the town. Hariboa asked him to carefully watch what was going to happen. So saying Hariboa began to grow tall. He grew nearly 20 feet high. At the same time the bulk of the body was extending breadth-wise. He grew nearly 15 feet wide. Vishnudas was watching it. At the sight of that giant-like formidable figure Vishnudas grew nervous and was frightened. He could not bear the unnatural phenomenon any longer. His brain began to reel. He thought that someone was cutting the ground underneath his feet. He looked upwards. He saw powerful light round about Hariboa's big face. Vishnudas was bewildered and the light dazzled his eyes. Vishnudas fell senseless on the ground.

After nearly fifteen minutes he came to himself and found himself alone in that field. He was at once on his legs and he took to flight through fright and anyhow reached a toll *naka*—booth, outside the town. While he was running pell-mell he tumbled down once or twice and his knees and some other parts of the body had sustained injuries. He spent the whole night at the *naka* and in the morning he went to his house.

While he was fomenting the injuries Hariboa again appeared and called him. Hariboa, in a jocular mood questioned Vishnudas, "How did you like last night's phenomenon? Do you want to see any more miracles?"

"Boa," Vishnudas said, "I need no further miracles. I am more than satisfied with the one I experienced last night."

"Why were you afraid last night? If you would have continued to be on your senses for all the time you would have been spiritually enlightened..."

Hariboa was extremely fond of children, who called him *mad Hari*. When little boys were on their way to their morning school Hariboa appeared before them and took to his heels. The boys ran after him in pursuit saying, "Mad Hari is running."

The scene was indeed very joyful. When the boys were tired with running after him they stopped. Hariboa also stopped at a small distance before them saying to them, "Well, come on, your fathers cannot catch me."

At this the boys followed the pursuit, Hariboa again went on running. And when he saw boys approaching him he at once jumped into the well and vanished. The boys kept waiting to see that Hariboa would erect his head out of the water but in vain. Hariboa kept himself submerged in water for several hours and the lookers-on went away in disappointment. Sometimes he remained under water from sunrise to sunset.

Sometime people jumped into the well to find out his trace but their attempts were never successful. He was never traced.

At times he lay on one side of his body on the ground in the temple of God Shiva. His hand served him as a pillow to support his head. Free from all movements of the body and with eyes always open without a twinkle he lay there without food, water or calls of nature continuously for a month or so.

Once he happened to wander in the village of Tembhurni. The village boys always shouted after him. One day, early in the morning the sons of some merchants confined him in a small room used as godown and the room was locked from outside. When the elderly persons knew this they reprimanded the boys who had done it and they unlocked the door with a view to release Hariboa. But they were surprised to find that he was not there. The room in which he was confined had no means of egress any way—no window, no opening nor even a small dent or hole. Escape from the room was physically impossible. With all this, Hariboa was not there. The news spread far and wide in no time. Villagers gathered together before that room. The whole atmosphere was in a state of wonderment.

There was no earthly explanation for Hariboa's escape.

When the group of villagers was discussing about the wonderful disappearance of Hariboa from the room, some persons came there from Pandharpur. They asked the people as to why they had gathered together. The people acquainted them with the miraculous incident. The persons said to them, "We saw that naked madman wandering in the Pandharpur bazaar in the afternoon."

It will not be out of place to note here that Pandharpur is some miles away from Tembhurni.

Sometimes Hariboa's behaviour was curious. He was once sitting in a grosser shop. There he found a purse full of some nuts whereof the oil of it if applied to the body causes eruptions. Hariboa took some nuts and crushed them with iron weights. The oil was extracted and, he forcibly rubbed it against tender parts of his body.

My father asked him, "What are you doing Boa?"

Hariboa replied that he was amusing himself; whereupon my father told him that the amusement would cost him dear; to which he only uttered God's name joyfully. My father thought that Hariboa would suffer from injurious eruptions on the body but when my father met him the next day he did not find even a black stain of that oil on his body much less any eruption.

After nearly three years he left Indapur and went to Baramati. From there he went to Pandharpur and Shinganapur where he passed six or seven years and finally he went to Phaltan. Owing to his residence there for 25 years people called him Hariboa Phaltankar.

When Hariboa arrived at Phaltan he began to enter any house, indiscriminately, throw away furniture there-from and caused, nuisance to the inhabitants. He wandered through streets in a state of nudity. He caused trouble to the way farers in various ways. He threw filth on their heads and soiled their clothes. Sometime he took a liking to play with boys and amuse them. People called him *mad Hari*. Sometimes people chased him but it was impossible to catch him. When he was closely followed by persons running after him, he at once jumped into the heap of thorny cactus and made the thorns his bed to lie down. He lay there for several days without either food or drink.

Some people once made a complaint to the police that Hariboa was causing nuisance to them. The police lodged a complaint against him. Hariboa never cared for his defence. When the magistrate tried to take his statement Hariboa did not utter a word. The magistrate thereupon convicted him and sentenced him to six months imprisonment.

The police unlocked him in jail and turned his face from him. No sooner did the police constable walk two or three paces than Hariboa caught hold of his shirt from behind saying, "Your father is out. Come and jail me."

The constable was rather in a confused state of mind. He doubted whether he had failed to lock the room. But when he took Hariboa to be put into the prison room he found the room locked. He unlocked the door and again forced Hariboa into the room. At this time he carefully locked the door and stood there for some minutes gazing at the prisoner. Then he turned his face and walked two or three paces, Hariboa again caught hold of his shirt saying, "Your father is again out. Where are you going without putting me into jail?"

The constable reported the matter to the administrator Mr. B. K. Bapat. He came to the jail room. He himself put Hariboa in jail, and then locked the room. He waited there for some time. But when he turned his back Hariboa was out. Being convinced of the mysterious powers of the prisoner he personally brought Sri Bapusaheb, the King of Phaltan to the jail room. Bapusaheb bowed down at the feet of Hariboa and begged to be excused for the trouble given to him. He thought that his mysterious escape from the locked-up room could not have happened unless he was a saint possessing great mystic powers.

Hariboa at Raja's earnest request accompanied him to his palace, but yet the riddle of his mysterious escape from the prison was never solved. And I may say that no physical science will be of any avail in solving it.

According to yoga philosophy no physical hindrance will bar a yogi to escape from any place, for he by yoga exercises gains power to assume *atomic form* and it goes without saying that an *atomic body* can have ingress, or egress anywhere.

Hariboa remained in the palace for a year or so. The Raja had given strict orders to the watchmen that they should always be alert so that Hariboa should not leave the palace. The Raja thought that the saint like Hariboa would be to him a guardian angel and would always look after his welfare.

But one day Hariboa disappeared from the palace and appeared in the village of Malthan a suburb of Phaltan. Phaltan and Malthan are divided by a small river between them. When the Raja knew that Hariboa was in Malthan he was sorry and he went to him and earnestly requested him to come again to stay in his palace. But his request did not get favourable response. Hariboa never went to the palace over again.

While Hariboa was in Phaltan people saw innumerable miracles performed by him. It is not possible to describe them all. I state only some of them. He cured many deceases only by means of his word.

There was one Brahmin in Phaltan. His name was Shridhar Gosavi. His son's name was Aba. The family was renowned for their art of singing. Once Aba had a dire attack of cholera and he was just on the point of death. No medicine could have any effect. All hopes of his recovery were lost. All the members of Aba's family prayed to Hariboa for his recovery. Hariboa came to Aba as if casually. Aba was lying down unconscious. Hariboa held his hand fast. The persons there tried to release it, but the grip was very hard and Aba's hand could not be released. Hariboa made Aba stand in that unconscious state. The persons nearby supported him. Hariboa then held him fast by his arms and then left him. Before he left the place, Hariboa took a little earth and applied it to Aba's forehead. Aba was made to lie down for a short time. Aba had a great motion, his stomach became empty. The result was that he soon opened his eyes and came to his senses. He said that he was very hungry, and asked for food.

His body was washed clean. He took a little food and water and then he had sound sleep. In a few days he was restored to his former health. All were wonderstruck by the fact that Hariboa saved Aba from the jaws of death. All were convinced about Hariboa's superhuman powers.

Hariboa sometimes was seen to have exercised his supreme powers even over nature.

The son of Aba Gosavi and son of Martandboa were once conversing together at the latter's house in Phaltan. In the course of conversation, son of Martandrao casually said, "This year there has been unusual delay in rainfall, and it has caused a great anxiety to the people. Now rain is absolutely required to undertake agricultural operations.

Otherwise there will be famine."

Hariboa casually came to the house where this conversation was going on. The son of Martandrao said to Hariboa, "The rains have been delayed, and it will be better if they now come early."

Hariboa heard it. His eyes became bloody red. It seemed as if they were to emit sparks of fire from them. He lifted a heavy iron rod from the ground and forcibly threw it at a distance. Hariboa looked very wild. At this Aba's son was terribly frightened and he ran away from that place. Son of Martandboa also ran away and hid himself in the rear compound of his house. Both the boys were overcome by terror.

Hariboa shouted, "You want rain! Isn't it? Have it then."

He then went to Aba's house. The door was chained from within. He tapped it twice or thrice. In a rage he said to the son of Aba, "You want rain? Here it is."

With these words he left Aba's house.

Seeing that Hariboa was away, Aba's son went to the son of Martandboa and narrated what happened at his house.

Both of them had never seen Hariboa in such a frightful form at any time before.

Evening approached. Flashes of lightning began to appear in the eastern portion of the sky, and they were followed by thunders. Then there was storm and torrential rains. Hariboa's word came true. People were rejoicing, their anxiety was removed and famine was averted. People were more devoted to Hariboa.

In Phaltan there was a boy named Dagadu. He was

aged six. Being lame from his nativity he could not walk. His parents therefore had a watch over him so that he should not crawl out of the house and sit on the street outside. One day he evaded their watch, came out of his house and was playing on the street among other boys. Hariboa while aimlessly wandering in the town came where these boys were playing. Through fear of him all the boys except the lame Dagadu hastily ran away to their respective homes. Dagadu could not run nor could he walk. He was confined to his place. Hariboa approached him, placed his hand on his head and said, "All your playmates have run away and why are you sitting here alone? Go home. Do not sit here. Run along!"

The boy not mindful of the fact that he was lame got up on his crippled legs and at once ran away from there.

From that day Dagadu began to walk and run like other boys. The inherent defect in his legs totally disappeared. It was a matter of great wonder to the people who knew this miraculous incident.

Majority of people of Phaltan and had the highest respect and great reverence for Hariboa. Yet there were some who considered him to be mad.

At that time there lived in Phaltan a pleader named Walimbe. His maid servant had once gone to the river for some work. Hariboa was there. He began to throw stones in the water of the river. A stone falling near the maid servant splashed water over her garment and made it wet. She went on abusing Hariboa and went home. She made a complaint to the pleader against Hariboa. The pleader got very much angry and in that mood he went to the river. He caught hold of Hariboa's hand and said, "Is this the hand by which you pelted the stone? I shall now see that it is fully punished." He then placed Hariboa's hand on a slab of stone and with another stone he gave a sound drubbing to it. The bruises and wounds caused thereby were profusely bleeding. At this two or three persons intervened for rescue and separated Hariboa's hand from the clutch of Walimbe. They took Hariboa to the administrator and informed him of the incident.

karbhari—administrator—asked Hariboa, "Who drubbed your hand?"

"*Vithal-Vithal.*" Hariboa just chanted the name of God.

The *karbhari* then asked Hariboa, his name, his father's name, surname, place of residence etc. for meeting the requirements of procedural law at the time of entertaining a complaint but to all the queries Hariboa's answer was, *Vithal-Vithal*.

As Hariboa was telling nothing more, *karbhari* also could do nothing more.

But exactly within a month of this cruel incident the pleader Walimbe died. People said that the pleader died owing to his cruelty to the great saint.

The foregoing two or three miracles are noted in a small pamphlet published very long ago. My father never referred to them; perhaps he did not know these incidents because they had taken place after Hariboa parted with my father at Indapur. After Hariboa left Indapur my father ceased to have a contact with him.

My brother however once told me one instance from the life of Hariboa. The miracle he performed was indeed a towering one.

A Brahmin was residing in a certain village. He was a

firm devotee of Hariboa. He used to see Hariboa every day.

On a certain day held sacred by the Hindus he saw Hariboa as usual. Some men of his village had gone to the holy place of Kashi which is otherwise known as *Benaras* which stands on the bank of the holy Ganges. Hariboa asked the Brahmin as to why he did not go to Kashi while others had gone there for bathing in the sacred Ganges. Brahmin replied that the men who had gone there were rich. He was poor and it was not possible for him to defray the travelling expenses.

To this Hariboa said, "If you are willing I shall take you to Kashi. Go back, put on your clothes and come here again."

The Brahmin went back put on his dress and again came to Hariboa. Hariboa held his hand and asked him to close his eyes till he asked him to open them. The Brahmin closed his eyes and very soon thereafter he lost all consciousness. After a while he heard Hariboa asking him to open his eyes. As soon as he opened them he was very much surprised to find that a big river with its vast expanse and grandeur was flowing before his eyes. Hariboa told him that it was the holy Ganges and that he should have a bath in it. The Brahmin bathed. Hariboa again asked him to see the God Vishweshwara in the temple just above a long flight of steps. The Brahmin ascended a number of steps, saw the presiding deity of the sacred temple, bowed down with deepest respect and again came to Hariboa.

Hariboa then told him that he would take him to Kolhapur in Deccan and asked him to close his eyes. Hariboa caught hold of his hand, and within a short- time he asked the Brahmin to open his eyes. The latter saw himself in a big temple yet unknown to him.

Hariboa told him, "This is the temple of the Goddess Laxmi. Bow to her."

This done, Hariboa said that he would show him Pandharpur. Again Hariboa held his hand. The Brahmin closed his eyes. When asked to open them he viewed before him the idol of Sri Vithal in the temple of Pandharpur. The Brahmin bowed down to the God Vithal with great reverence. Hariboa then brought him back to his village which he had left at 8 in the morning along with Hariboa. When he came back to the village it was 11 a.m. In this way, a long journey of thousands of miles which would require some days to travel was finished merely within three hours! No one would believe in the ordinary course of nature but this miracle has actually taken place on the strength of vast yogic powers which Hariboa had acquired. Ancient Indian yoga philosophy lays down rules for acquiring such supernatural powers. Hence I am prone to believe in such miraculous deeds provided I know them either personally or from the reports of the most reliable persons.

Hariboa was a great yogi who had acquired tremendous occult powers which enabled him to perform great miraculous deeds. It seems that he wanted people to guard them against blind faith and to create in them a real faith. Hariboa never focused on his miraculous acts. He in fact asked his disciples to keep mum about these miraculous happenings.

That is why I have referred only to some of them in this book. The reader is at liberty to draw any conclusion he likes about this mystic saint. But here in the Deccan all sections of the public are unanimous in recognising him to have been the greatest yogi and saint.

Full twenty-five years had passed since Hariboa came to Phaltan. It was now time for him to end his earthly career. In *Shake* 1820 there was a great festival of *Ratha Saptami*. Many persons came to Hariboa. They were singing *bhajans*. The Raja Nirabalkar of Phaltan was also among these persons. A great feast was given to the people in the town. People raised loud shouts of Hariboa's name and took food. Hariboa, however, did not eat anything. But Gopaldas, a firm devotee of Hariboa made him to partake a little of it. Narayanboa Phaltankar a famous singer made *kirtan* and all ceremonies in connection with the festival were duly performed. The people being thus engaged in the festival, Hariboa went into a trance. His disciples began to serve him as usual. One of the disciples felt his feet cold. Immediately a doctor was called for. He came and bowed down to Hariboa. He examined him. He could not utter a word through intense grief. With a sob and sigh he declared that Hariboa was no more.

The news came to the people as a bolt from the blue. The sad news of Hariboa's demise spread far and wide like wild fire. Crowds of people flocked there to have a last sight of Hariboa's figure. Raja Nimbalkar ordered to make arrangement of his Samadhi. Many masons were engaged to cut stones to shape. The work was speedily done.

He was profusely garlanded and his body closed in clothes. After other due formalities the body was taken in long procession.

The procession with thousands of people of all castes

and creeds was headed by a staff of musicians. The tunes of trumpets in the band and the sound of *tashas*—drums—and other instruments were resounding in the sky. Hariboa's body was thus brought to the place where it was to be interred.

In the pit a seat for Hariboa was prepared. The body was placed in a sitting pasture. Two burning lamps were kept on both his sides. The place of *samadhi* was closed and a stone on which embossed feet of Hariboa were carved was placed on the top of the structure in which the saint's body was buried.

In this way this great saint, himself a nude all throughout his life, spent his whole life in obliging the people in various ways, ended his earthly career on the 11th day of the bright half of the month of *Magh* according to the Hindu calendar. I was then 25 or 26 years old.

A feeling of sorrow was sometimes uppermost in my mind for not having personally seen Hariboa at anytime in my life though I could have seen him. Recently a very grand and beautiful temple is erected over his *Samadhi*—sacred remains. If not in his life time yet I had a mind to pay a visit to his sacred *samadhi*. Accordingly a couple of years back I visited the place.

The temple and its surrounding landscape at once captivated my mind. There is a grand assembly hall. It is open on all sides. The ground within the compound of the temple is extensive. There are *dharmashalla* just in the vicinage of the temple where pilgrims and visitors put up for taking their food and rest. There is a well in the compound. It has excellent water. A water pipe adjoins it. Beyond the temple compound there is a small river and beyond it the town of Phaltan stands on its bank. It was the capital of the King of Phaltan State but now absorbed in the Government of Maharashtra.

The situation of *samadhi* is charming and it's surrounding atmosphere calm. It is within the precincts of Malthan. When a man steps on that sacred ground, his mind at once becomes calm and divested of all worldly cares. Sweet tunes of birds occasionally add to the charm of that secluded place.

I went there in the morning and returned from there in the afternoon. During that time I saw innumerable men, women, boys and girls visiting the *samadhi* temple and bowing down to the *samadhi* in reverence. In spite of these visitors, gravity and calmness of that place did not seem to have been affected in the least.

I put my head on Hariboa's *paduka*—memorial footwear—and then looked at his big photo-picture placed in front thereof. The reverential awe of that sacred place and Hariboa's grand image appearing in the photo brought tears of joy in my eyes. I said to myself, *'This is the God-like man whose divine word totally changed the aspect of our family and it was he whose favour on our family brought us in the fore. But for his grace we could have been nowhere.'*

Afterwards I took a round about the temple. Just behind the temple I observed a slab of stone. It is said that it had been Hariboa's place of resort. In all the seasons of the year he had taken a liking to sit on this stone in scorching heat of summer, severe cold of winter or heavy rains of monsoons. Persons therefore consider this stone as sacred and they worship it. It's association with Hariboa has got sacred immortality. It has got the status of God.

Time was fleeting. Time to catch the bus was fast approaching but the charm of the place was preventing me from taking my steps to the motor stand. Anyhow I left the place and got the bus. My mind, however, was hovering round about the temple. The bus started, my mind lingering behind. The bus gained speed. It came near the temple. I took its last view. It was vividly appearing against the golden sky. Our bus was running fast, the temple seemed running fast in opposite direction. In a short time, that view also disappeared. But to my inner mind the loving image of Hariboa was vividly presenting itself, in the course of my homeward journey.

Bhapkar Maharaj

A glance at the dilapidated building reminds me of a crowd of events of more than half a century past. Almost all the fine stones of the front wall of that splendid edifice are dislocated from their original places. But even in their present plight they testify to the glory of the magnificent building before its dilapidation. I think that the person who erected that structure as if was talking to me. All the signs showing that the building had once given shelter to the human beings and domestic animals are obliterated and they now rest in oblivion. When we look at the dilapidated condition of that building we are fully convinced about the fact that the enmity between man and death is eternal. There is invariable concomitance between man and death. In this very building one individual was living about more than eighty years past.

The building was then erect and the individual happy.

This ramshackle structure is very near our house in Karjat of Ahmednagar District. It is called Bhapkar *wada*. Our way to the Bazaar and to our fields passes by it.

Last year I was passing by that *wada*, when curiously enough I heard some one remarking that the *wada* was haunted by ghosts. I was indeed sorry to hear the remark. I was so to say shocked to hear it. I was rather upset. I pitied the man for not knowing the past grandeur of that *wada*. I was sorry to see that present generation thinks only of the present and future but not of the past in the least. I had however present and past in my mind.

Once that *wada* was a place of human habitation and I considered it as a holy temple but now stray cattle were making all sort of nuisance there! The stones were lying down at random. Earth was mixed with mortar. Almost all other landmarks were buried down underground. Yet I remembered them all. My memory was fresh as respect to the past history of the *wada*.

Here I am giving a story of an individual who spent his early days in that house and who subsequently chanced to have a different turn in life and became a Yogi and a great saint. His name in early years was Laxman. Later on people used to call him Bhapkar Maharaj.

In the house referred to above he was staying with his elder step-brother called Nana Bhapkar. Beside this house of their ownership they had landed property under well-irrigation. Nana looked to the management of this property. The relations of these brothers were not smooth. The younger brother's education was therefore neglected. Anyhow he went upto standard V in the primary school and left it. If Laxman wanted even a paltry amount of money Nana never paid him even a trifling coin. In these circumstances Laxman once took some sacred sheets of silver whereon images of some Gods from Hindu pantheon were embossed and sold them away in the market for satisfying his own needs. Nana came to know about this incident. He got very angry; he scolded Laxman for this act and plainly told him that he would no longer feed him.

In this way Laxman lost his fraternal support and he saw no one on earth to support him. But at the very time plenty of carrot was lying in his room. Day and night he ate it to satisfy his hunger. Continuous diet of carrot upset his stomach and he suffered from dysentery. His stepbrother did not care to give him medical help. Laxman was confined to bed. He had grown so week that he was quite unable to move from his bed. He grew serious. He himself thought that he would not recover from that illness.

In this helpless and hopeless condition he was lying down on his bed in a dreamy state. It was moon-light. He heard a knock at the door. He slowly went crawling and unchained the door. He saw a human figure entering his room. The person had a bag on his shoulder. Placing the bag on the ground he said, "Laxman, I have brought twenty four kilogram of Jowar for you. Do not eat carrot hereafter. Eat fresh bread of Jowar. The grain which I have brought will be sufficient to cure you and regain strength. As soon as the stock of grain is over you should come to the village Ajanuj and come to the *math* of Govindboa."

With these words the man left the room and rode away.

Laxman was surprised at the dramatic appearance of that stranger at such an odd hour at night. Many questions he put to himself, 'Who was that man? How did he know of my illness? Why should he have taken interest for me? How did he know that I was living on carrots? Why should he have supplied Jowari to me? And why should he have invited me to Ajanuj?' He had no answer to these questions. He could not solve the mystery.

By the time the stock of Jowari was consumed Laxman was fully cured and he had had strength to walk to Ajanuj, a distance of about 25 miles from Karjat. Accordingly he went there, inquired about Govindboa's *math*. A villager showed it to him. He entered, and saw Govindboa. He at once recognized him, as he was the same person who had supplied Jowari to him when he was ill and had invited him to Ajanuj.

Govindboa was a bachelor. By yoga practices he was endowed with supernatural powers. He was a seer. At Ajanuj he had with his mental eye seen the condition of Laxman at the distance of twenty-five miles and came to his help.

Govindboa initiated Laxman into yoga practices and asked him to go to the bank of the river Narmada for exercising yoga.

As advised by him Laxman spent twelve years on the bank of the Narmada. He completed his practice there and he returned to his native place at Karjat. He had then acquired supernatural powers.

Now people began to call him Laxman Maharaj or Bhapkar Maharaj.

When Bhapkar Maharaj went to the Narmada, his stepbrother Nana mortgaged the ancestral property at Karjat and went to reside at Mandavgan in Srigonda.

When the Maharaj knew this after his return from the Narmada he had no source of income for his livelihood. He therefore went to reside at Vairag in Sholapur District. By that time he was married. His wife was from a village not far off from Vairag.

Bhapkar Maharaj brought a suit for redemption against the mortgagee. The sub-judge in whose court the proceedings were going on was thinking of dismissing Maharaj's suit with a view that the mortgaged lands should go to his own friend free of charge. When Maharaj came to know of this, he remarked, "My cause is true; if in spite of this the sub-judge thinks of deciding my case against me I will send him away to the sea-shore."

Some one reported this remark to the sub-judge; on learning it he came to Bhapkar Maharaj and asked him if he made such a remark. Bhapkar Maharaj replied, "Yes, I have remarked that way."

"But how do you think that I would do injustice in the case?" asked the sub-judge.

Maharaj said, "If it is really so you have no reason to fear."

But the sub-judge had not, however, changed his original intention. Within a week he was transferred to a place near seashore. His successor was very strict and of judicious mind, decreed redemption in that suit. He ordered that the possession of the suit lands should be given to plaintiff on his paying the decrial amount to the defendant.

On taking over possession of his lands Maharaj used to come to Karjat at the harvest time for recovering his share in the produce. For that he had to stay there for at least two months or even more.

It was in 1902 that he first visited my house. He opened up a theological question for discussion. We discussed it in such a way that much interest was created thereby. Though I was acquainted with him from some years before that, yet it was from 1902 that I had close contact with him and it lasted for the next fourteen years. During this period I derived immense benefit from his talk with me in matters sublime.

After his study of yoga he visited many places in Southern India. His disciples and followers were countless in number. Among them were doctors, pleaders, *Deshmukhs* and *Deshpandes*, and even government officials, all belonging to the intellectual class. They revered him as God. Maharaj never asked for help from any one and in any form. He also never cared to see how his family was being maintained. His disciples voluntarily visited his house in his absence and made inquiries with his wife as to the wants of the family. In this way all the wants were supplied by his devotees behind his back. He also never inquired as to how the family affairs were managed, as the income from his lands was more than sufficient to defray the expenses of the family.

When Maharaj was in a state of trance his body sometimes seemed hanging in horizontal position nearly one or two feet above the ground. Thus he used to make his body as light as cotton. A layman would deem it a wonder, or an intelligent man may consider it as an impossibility, but that a yogi possesses such powers is a fact. Patanjali *muni*—sage—has given explanation of this feat in his *Yoga-darshana in Sutra 42 of Vibhutipada*.

According to him man's body is made of *Akashatatwa* i.e. sky element has taken the form of human body. If a man makes deep meditation on this element, he can make his body as light as cotton and can pass from one place to another through sky. So there is no wonder if Bhapkar Maharaj used to keep his body hanging when he was in a state of trance.

Maharaj had once gone to Hyderabad in Deccan. At that time there was a Muslim saint in that town. He used to sit on water and say his prayers. This feat had gathered many a disciple around him. Fame of Bhapkar Maharaj as a yogi had spread everywhere in the town. The Muslim saint therefore sent his disciple for giving him invitation.

Bhapkar Maharaj went to the Muslim saint, accompanied by many of his followers. The saint received Maharaj with due respect.

After formal talk the Muslim saint said to Bhapkar Maharaj, "It is now time for me to say my prayers; I wish to show you how I do it. Please therefore wait and see."

Then the saint descended the flight of steps in a well. Maharaj followed him. The saint asked his disciple to bring a square piece of cloth. He brought it and handed it to the saint, who threw it on the well-water. The saint afterwards sat on that cloth and began to offer his prayers. Maharaj was standing on the steps and looking at the saint.

Then the saint asked the Maharaj with a little pride, "Can you do this?"

"Why do you require the cloth between the water and your body?" The Maharaj questioned him in return.

"How is it possible to sit without cloth?" was the saint's query.

Bhapkar Maharaj at once jumped on water, sat thereon as if on ground and said, "This is the way."

At this the Muslim saint lost all his pride and in humble submission bowed down at the feet of the Maharaj.

Bhapkar Maharaj then explained to the saint as to how he could sit on water without taking support of cloth underneath his body. The saint offered thanks to the Maharaj for giving him valuable directions. The Maharaj took his leave and left the place.

Once, the Bhapkar Maharaj had been to Karmala in Sholapur District. Mr. Nulkar was the *Mamledar*—collector—of Karmala. He invited the Maharaj to his place of residence. The Maharaj went there. Two Mohammedan police officers—one sub-inspector and another a head constable—were sitting at the collector's house when the Maharaj went there. While all of them were talking the palanquin containing the idol of Sri Ram was being taken in procession. It stopped before the collector's house. The collector went out and put one rupee in palanquin. After receiving a cocoanut by way of favour, he came back. The Maharaj asked him to break the cocoanut and distribute the pieces of kernel to all. The collector offered two or three pieces to either of the police officers sitting there.

They said, "We do not want the favour of your God, we want the favour of the Maharaj."

Then the Maharaj took six pieces of cocoanut kernel from Mr. Nulkar and gave them to the two police officers, three pieces each.

The police officers had kept them in their pockets. They went to their respective homes. When they put their hands into their pockets, they found eggs instead of pieces of cocoanut.

They at once hastened to the collector's house where the Maharaj was yet sitting. They informed the collector and the Maharaj of the miracle about eggs. The Maharaj said to them, "You wanted my favour; you did not want Hindu God's favour. So your Allah has given you what you wanted. You must be satisfied with what you got."

The Mohammedans wondered at what had happened and they returned to their abodes.

Bhapkar Maharaj was expert in yoga practices. Once, he had given instructions to a certain person in exercises in breathing. He had given him particular warning that the breath must not be retained inside for more than a certain time. Duration of such retention should on no account be lengthened. But the person, in spite of these clear instructions, once retained his breath longer than he was advised. The result was that the wind got a different passage in the body and he had a big hump on his back. He could not walk straight. The body was bent, and he had sharp pain in his back. Bhapkar Maharaj had been wandering from place to place. His whereabouts could not be traced. In these circumstances the person had to suffer from this pain for nearly six months.

When the person saw the Maharaj the latter scolded him for having transgressed his instructions. The person earnestly requested him that he should be cured. The Maharaj asked him to take an oath that he would not practise the breathing exercise any further. The person took an oath and said that he would not.

Then the Maharaj asked him to take breath and retain it for a time. He did so. The Maharaj placed his finger on a certain point on his back and pressed it. Air inside the body began to make noise. The Maharaj repeated the process four to five times, each time the bulk of the hump coming less. Ultimately the hump entirely disappeared and the back restored to its former state. It needs no saying that the person absolutely abandoned the idea of becoming a Yogi.

Once Maharaj and myself were sitting together conversing on some topics. I casually asked him if he would kindly give me instructions in *hathayog*.

He replied, *"Hathayog* is not essential for you. The way you are following is smooth and free from pitfalls. Your path being safe why should you wish to go through the trammels of that intricate yoga? I shall, however, give you those instructions as you desire provided you will not practice *pranayam*—yogic breathing—etcetera dealt with by that system and will not impart instructions to others."

Then, after three or four days passed, he gave me full instructions in the practice of several *asana* and *pranayam* according to that of yoga. He apprized me of their utility. He did not; however forget to repeat his warning previously given to me.

Maharaj practiced *rajyog* and *hathayog* both, and he being expert in them was a yogi of the first order. When Maharaj was at his home in Vairag, he daily went into *samadhi* for five times; but when he was outside he did it thrice.

When he was at Karjat many persons came to see him at the close of the day, and asked him to deliver a speech on a certain subject.

Before beginning to speak it was his practice to close his

eyes and sit motionless for nearly five minutes. Swami Vivekananda is said to have similar practice before commencing his speech before the audience. When Bhapkar Maharaj closed his eyes he at once went into trance and he remained in the state of *samadhi* for five or six minutes. When he came to himself, he had copious perspiration. After wiping it off he began his speech. He went on speaking for three or four hours without break. He used to speak on any subject suggested by any one. I have heard his speeches on Physics, Chemistry, Medical science, Astronomy, Astrology, Yoga, Dharma, Vedanta and other scientific subjects. He expressed his thoughts in simple but beautiful language interlarded with appropriate similes, which made the audience spell bound. One famous man had remarked about him that an orator of his type cannot be found even among ten thousand men.

Bhapkar Maharaj left school when he was in fifth standard. After leaving school he had not read any books. It was therefore a mystery as to when and how he had acquired vast knowledge about all the subjects. But I had got a solution of that mystery in one of his speeches.

While giving a lecture on Indian Philosophy he said, "When one gets acquainted with the Almighty God, there remains nothing unknown."

Bhapkar Maharaj was a living example of this aphorism. In course of time I happened to read the yoga *sutras* of Patanjali. I found a *sutra* relevant to this subject—'when a man concentrates on three *parinamas*—effects viz. *dharma, lakshan* and *avastha* he acquires knowledge of the past and present events and events of future dawn on his vision. The above *sutra* has its place in the *vibhutipada* of

'Paatanjala Yogadarshana'.

One Mr. Anjangaokar was an officer in the survey department at Pune; he was a disciple of Bhapkar Maharaj. He and some other great personages requested him to speak on Dharma in general, and they arranged his lecture at Anand Ashram in Pune. *Lokmanya* Bal Gangadhar Tilak and Prof. Bhanu of Fergusson College were among the audience. Lokmanya was acquainted with the Maharaj and he had great respect for him. The Maharaj began his speech at 6 in the evening. At 9 he was about to finish it but the audience requested him to continue. The Maharaj then spoke for an hour more and then stopped. In the end *Lokmanya* Tilak remarked, "People in Pune and thereabouts know not much about the Maharaj but I am well acquainted with him. From the way he delivered his lecture all of you must have been convinced about his greatness. As it is now high time to disperse I may say in short about him that the Maharaj is the present Raamdas." (Raamdas was great saint and *karmayogi* in Maharashtra some 300 years ago.)

On being invited the Maharaj had visited the resident place of Prof. Bhanu. The latter showed him a booklet भगवद्गीतेचा उपसंहार—Epilogue of Bhagavad-Gita—written by him. The Maharaj on seeing it for some time remarked, "Your view about Gita is merely quite superficial... Read Gita carefully over again and you will find out your mistakes."

This was followed by a question by Bhanu to the Maharaj, "Unless anyone shows us one's supernatural powers how we could recognize him as a saint?"

"Even if a saint abstains from exhibiting such powers,"

The Maharaj replied, "he does not lose his status as a saint."

There was a pause for sometime. The Maharaj then asked Bhanu if he wants to see something supernatural about which he will not find any explanation. He asked Bhanu to shut his eyes. Bhanu closed his eyes. The Maharaj immediately asked him to open them. Bhanu did so and to his great surprise he saw before him a heap of sugar candy. He was struck with wonder. Maharaj himself ate a little bit from that heap and asked Bhanu to taste it. After Bhanu tasted it Maharaj asked him again to close his eyes and open them again. In a twinkle of an eye Bhanu saw that the heap of sugar has disappeared—not a particle was to be seen there.

After a little pause Maharaj said, "Well Mr. Bhanu," who was rather wonderstruck by the strange event, "is it not wonderful that the sugar candy appeared and disappeared in some moments? I tell you that an intelligent person like you will do this within six months, provided you have firm faith and tenacity."

Bhanu then requested the Maharaj to advise him and initiate him in that field. Bhapkar Maharaj replied, "Make a firm resolve about it and then shall see."

Bhanu then wrote some letters to the Maharaj but the letter was ever silent.

We were once sitting together at Karjat, when a *marwadi*—the a person from the community from Marawad, Rajasthan, runs business especially of grocery shop—came to see the Maharaj. He was accompanied by his daughter aged about twelve or thirteen. His place of residence was nearly eighty miles distant from Karjat. Every day crosses of marking nut appeared on her body.

Her body was therefore ever swollen. Sometimes a nook of a string came round her neck to strangle it. When the girl was taking her food, excrement appeared in her dish. Her father did everything to stop this occult trouble for nearly two years and a half but to no good. This cost him a lot of money. Then someone told him that Bhapkar Maharaj would end their trouble and hence the *marwadi* had been to the Maharaj.

The Maharaj made inquiries as to where he came and why. The *marwadi* told him the sad story about his daughter and showed him the black crosses all over her body. These crosses were nearly one inch apart from one another. The Maharaj asked us to see her body. We indeed pitied the girl who was suffering from that trouble for more than a couple of years. Then the Maharaj said to the marwadi, "All this trouble will be over from today; you can go home quite care-free."

After the *marwadi* took his departure the Maharaj then said, "This is a sort of witchcraft called *bhanamati*. I am aware of many such instances. But crosses will not hereafter appear on her body."

The *marwadi*—father of the girl remained at Karjat for nearly a week. He daily used to come to the Maharaj in the morning and evening.

On the 8th day the Maharaj asked him if fresh crosses appeared on his daughter's body or if any other mischief appeared to his view. The *marwadi* replied in the negative, and added that the previous crosses which had caused swelling on the girl's body had totally disappeared. The Maharaj then assured him that his daughter would not suffer any more from such a mischief, and that he may go home.

The *marwadi* said, "I am greatly obliged by you. What should I pay for requiting these obligations?" We were there near the Maharaj. We told the *marwadi* that the Maharaj do not accept anything for obliging others. The *marwadi* and his daughter then paid their respects to the Maharaj and wended their way homeward.

This incident, viz the cure of *marwadi*'s daughter by Bhapkar Maharaj only by means of his word had sometimes been haunting my mind. I found the solution of this in *Pantajala Yoga-darshana*. The desire of a truthful man expressed in words accompanied with his will power creates circumstances favourable to the fulfilment of such a desire and thus by his words are realized. A yogi possesses such a will power and therefore his words never prove unfructuous. Bhapkar being a great yogi his word in case of the *marwadi*'s daughter came true and she was free from the trouble consequent on *bhanamati*—witchcraft).

Once, Bhapkar Maharaj had his stay at Ropla in Sholapur district for nearly three weeks. He daily used to speak on some topic suggested by the villagers who were present in the evening at the place where the Maharaj had lodged. The Post Master there was regularly present among the visitors. He had no issue either male or female. He was a firm devotee of the Maharaj. He had a mind to question the Maharaj as to what remedy he would suggest for having an issue but he had no courage to ask him such a question. After eight or ten days Maharaj said that he must leave the village very soon and go elsewhere; but the villagers pressed him to prolong his stay. Thus he remained there for ten days more.

On a Sunday afternoon the Maharaj abruptly left Ropla without taking leave of the village people and went to a village nearly fourteen miles distant from Ropla. At that time the Post master had gone to a field for a *Hurda* party. When he returned at 5 in the evening he came to know that the Maharaj had left the village in the afternoon, he became somewhat uneasy. He took his supper and went to bed. The image of the Maharaj was before his mental eye. He closed the outer door of his premises by chaining it from within. He then chained the door of the room in which he had to sleep. Time was fleeting. He was drowsy. He thought that someone was tapping the door of his room. The Post Master asked, "Who is it?"

"I am Lakshman," was the response. He therefore got up and unchained the door; and to his great surprise he saw the Maharaj standing before him. The thought that Maharaj had left his village has totally disappeared. Maharaj entered the room. He asked the Post Master's wife to take her seat in front of him. He put a cocoanut into the *pallu* of the sari she was wearing, and told the Post Master that his wife should worship that cocoanut every day and that by Almighty's grace a son will be born to her within a year. So saying the Maharaj left the room.

The Post Master and his wife being joyed at the prediction made by the Maharaj were for some time talking together. The Post Master got up to chain the room. At the same time he thought the outer door of the house must be opened as the Maharaj had recently gone out. So he went to the outer door, but he found that its chain was not removed. He questioned to himself as to how the Maharaj must have gone out as there was no other way of egress. He was rather puzzled by this dilemma. If the appearance of the Maharaj was a dream, the cocoanut actually given by him was evidence to believe this conjecture. The Post Master was at a loss to solve the mystery.

He went out and saw some of the villagers and asked them whether the Maharaj was seen by any one at about 10 at night. Everyone replied in the negative. They were all wonderstruck.

Some six or seven persons resolved to go to the village to which the Maharaj had gone. The Post Master accompanied by these persons accordingly reached that village at 5 before dawn. They found the Maharaj playing chess. On inquiry they came to know that the previous evening Maharaj had not left the place even for a moment. They told the Maharaj about the incident which took place in the Post Master's house, but without uttering a single word he only smiled. The party returned. The Post Master's wife gave birth to a son within a year.

The Maharaj had acquired the Siddhi called *Bhutajaya*. When he was at Ropla another mystic occurrence took place. Some persons were sitting together near the Maharaj at about sunset. Among them was a person who was engaged to worship a deity in a certain temple in that village. He was about to leave the place where the Maharaj was sitting in the assemblage. The Maharaj asked him the reason why he was going. The reply was that he was going to purchase oil for lighting a lamp in the temple.

The Maharaj said, "We have heard that some saints had in the past made use of water instead of oil for lighting lamps. Let us therefore go to the temple and use water as a substitute for oil." The Maharaj with some persons went to the temple, asked the person- the worshipper of deity- to pour water in the lamp-pot, and ignite the wick with a match. The person did so and to the surprise of all the lamp was lighted. The lamp had been burning as if oil was put in the lamp-pot. Thus the Maharaj did on account of the Siddhi called *Bhutajaya*.

Bhapkar Maharaj had also the power of reading the minds of others. I have not, at least, come across with anyone else having such a power. Here I give my own experience about it. One afternoon he was explaining to me some cardinal principles of Vedanta. He said that the principles of Dharma, Dnyana and yoga primarily stood on equal footing. 'Ahimsa', 'Satya' are not hard and fast doctrines. In their practical use, they are subject to exceptions. If the use of Ahimsa or truth would result in a calamity, it must be avoided and himsa and untruth should be used instead. He quoted many instances from Manu Smriti, Dnyaneshwari and worldly transaction in support of what he said. But while he was discussing on this subject I was little bit inattentive. Some 70 or 80 labourers were working in my field where I had to go to make payment of their daily wages. This idea was revolving in my mind. The Maharaj at once said to me, "Give attention to what I am saying; There is yet ample time for you to go to the field." So saying he smiled and continued to speak on the subject of discourse.

Both of us were once sleeping in an open yard adjacent to our house, as it was summer time. I was lying down with my eyes closed. Some vivid scene was before my mental eye. The Maharaj tapped my shoulder and asked me if a particular scene was before my closed eyes. As he exactly referred to the scene, I had, of course to give an affirmative reply. Then we got up on our beds, had some talk on Dhyanayog and then retired to rest. There are several instances of his knowing what was passing in the mind of others.

Once, while Bhapkar Maharaj was sitting in our house the collector and the sub judge came to see him. There were also many persons present. Some one questioned him whether a person who had attained salvation while living would again fall down if he would die in Dakshinayana or on the day of no moon day.

The Maharaj replied, "The principle is that as soon as a man acquires knowledge of the universal soul, he at once gets moksha. His further actions are just like fried seed which is void of germinating power. The liberated person is free from the effects of either merit or demerit.'

At this time we had not the idea that he himself would soon end his earthly career thereafter. The Maharaj knew the exact day of his end. He called his son and said to him, "Now the parrot would soon fly away from its cage. I have already enlightened you on matters divine. I have not left you in the dark."

On a certain day hereafter he had gone out to take a walk. His son was with him. He pointed to a particular place and said to his son, "How beautiful this place is. I think that I should have my permanent stay here."

This was indeed a prior intimation of his death. As the Maharaj had in his life, attained the highest goal of life viz. salvation he never showed any anxiety about his family affairs. He had thrown that burden on the Almighty

God and led his life in divine joy and happiness. It was not possible for him to be fettered by the shackles of worldly pleasures. He was ever ready to meet the last moment of his life.

Three or four days after his talk with his son, the Maharaj asked him as to when *uttarayana* begins. His reply was that it would begin after a couple of days. Bheeshmacharya had also been waiting till the advent of *uttarayana* for meeting his death. It is said that a person dying in *uttarayana* goes to heaven.

The Maharaj had high fever. Doctors came from Barshi and Sholapur to see him. The thermometer showed normal temperature. Inspite of high fever the thermometer could not record it. The doctors were rather confused as they could not find the reason why the thermometer could not record the high temperature. The Maharaj said with a smile, "Well doctor, my temperature is not such as to be recorded in your thermometers."

The doctors could not therefore diagnose the cause of such peculiar heat in the body of the Maharaj and they therefore went to their respective places.

The holy day of *ekadashi* dawned. It was a bright fortnight. On this memorable day the Maharaj, as per his foresight and prediction, surrendered his last breath to heaven. The individual soul merged into the universal soul viz. the Almighty God, and was therefore free from further births and deaths.

From this association, I can say, I got much precious aid in matters divine and it is therefore hard to forget him and his advice in those matters as long as life exists.

GALAXY OF SAINTS

Ganapati Mhaskar

A devotee acquires some supernatural powers by virtue of his firm devotion to his desired deity and on the strength of these powers he can work some miracles for which human intellect fail to find any earthly explanation.

Shri Ganapati Mhaskar was a firm devotee of the God Sri Ganesh. He was resident of Shirgaon a village nearly three miles from Ratnagiri in Konkan. Born a pauper he was anyhow passing his days in extreme difficulties. When he was twenty years of age he had a necessity to perform some religious rites, but he had no sufficient money for that purpose. He felt extremely sorry for his poverty.

At this time he recollected a Marathi verse in which it was related that God Moraya (Ganesh) of Morgaon on the banks of the Karla river fulfils the desires of those that go on pilgrimage to that holy place. He therefore thought to himself, *'If the God Moraya is such as described in the above verse, why not go to him and get free from poverty?'*

He did not; however know where Morgaon was situated. He made enquiry about it and then he came to Mumbai and then went to Thane. In those days there were railway lines only between Mumbai and Thane, and not beyond. From Thane he went to Pune and then to Morgaon on foot, for he had no money to undertake that journey in any conveyance.

Not being acquainted with any one at Morgaon, he had his stay in an *ovari*—arcade within the premises of the temple of the God Moraya. He ate ground-nuts and fried grams to satisfy his hunger and in his mind offered his prayer to Moraya to remove his poverty.

At that time there was a great saint at Morgaon. He happened to see this boy sitting alone in the arcade. He asked the boy as to why he came there. Ganapatiboa explained to him his purpose of visiting the place. The saint was moved by his impoverished condition and asked him to recite a certain mantra for 21 days without taking food. So according to the saint's advice Ganapatiboa recited the mantra for the stated period and while doing so he ate only ground-nuts just to satisfy his hunger.

On the night of the 21st day he had a dream, in which he heard a voice, *'While taking a round about the temple you will find my golden image, take it and go to Mumbai.'*

He apprised the saint of this dream. The saint said to him that after finding the image he should go to Mumbai and see what takes place there; but that in the meanwhile he should go on worshipping the golden image of Sri Moraya with firm devotion.

His dream was realised. While taking a round about the temple he found the golden image of Sri Ganesh on his way. His joy knew no bounds. He went straightaway to his Guru and showed him the image. He took his permission and left Morgaon for Mumbai.

After going to Mumbai he had his stay in the Anant Rish's wadi. Every morning he was absorbed in the worship of the image with devout mind.

No sooner than a couple of days passed then he had a dream in which he got the following intimation, 'Two persons will come to see you tomorrow and question you about their ships. Tell them that their ships with cargo will arrive at Mumbai harbour safe from foreign land on Wednesday afternoon. You should demand from them what you want.'

The two owners of those ships had been restless as the ships had not arrived at the Mumbai harbour in due time. They both had simultaneously the same dream in which they were told that they should go to Ganapatiboa in Anant Rishi's wadi and ask him about their ships. He will free them from their anxiety.

The next morning the two owners of the ships met together and talked about their dreams regarding the same topic.

As the ships were loaded with goods worth some hundred of thousand rupees the owners of those ships felt very much anxiety, and had become restless. They therefore went to the Anant Rishi's wadi in accordance with their dreams and there they inquired about Ganapatiboa Mhaskar. Some persons told them that one Ganapati Mhaskar from Ratnagiri had arrived there and was staying on the 1st floor, and that they would find him there. They went there and saw Ganapatiboa engrossed in worshipping the God Ganesh. When they arrested his attention he at once questioned them, "Your ships are missing; is it not?"

The owners of the ships were greatly astonished at this question. They asked themselves as to how Ganapatiboa put such a point-blank question without being told about missing ships. Again Ganapatiboa said, "You need not to be anxious. Your ships had to face a storm but they are safe and they will arrive at the Mumbai harbour on the coming Wednesday in the afternoon."

Ganapatiboa paused a while and then he questioned them, "If your ships arrive at the harbour as I say what will you offer Lord Ganesh?"

"One hundred thousand!" they replied and then took their departure.

The owners of ships were anxiously waiting for the coming Wednesday. At last that day dawned. To their great surprise the ships entered the harbour exactly at 3 P.M. as was stated by Ganapatiboa.

The ship owners' joy knew no bounds. Loss of ships and goods therein would be a loss of several hundreds of thousand rupees; but Ganapatiboa's word has saved them from that immense loss. They therefore hastened to the abode of Ganapatiboa and placed before him *hundis*—bonds—worth one hundred thousand rupees.

Ganapatiboa had left home with a keen desire to be free from poverty. He had firm faith that God Sri Moraya would satisfy his desire. With this faith he had gone to Morgaon. There he was guided by a saintly person. Sri Moraya had told him in his dream that his desire would be fulfilled. When a man has keen desire to obtain anything and offer his prayers to God, he helps him to acquire it.

As soon as Ganapatiboa got one hundred thousand rupees, the greed for money totally disappeared from his mind. He felt that as he was under Sri Moraya's favour, Moraya would certainly look to his needs. He therefore spent the amount in building a fine temple of Ganapati at his native place and distributing the remaining amount in charity. He thereafter left his native place and went on journeying from place to place. In the course of his journey he again went to Morgaon. He had his stay there for four or five years in serving the God.

Then he went to Gwalior. The Scindia, knowing Ganapatiboa's prowess as a saint gave him two villages in Malwa as gift. The income of those villages was nearly twelve thousand rupees per year. These villages had been for several years the property of descendants of Ganapatiboa. Some authentic persons from that side told me that when Ganapatiboa expired, he left behind him twenty hundred thousand of rupees and the two gift villages which annually fetched an income of Rs.12000.

Ganapatiboa is an instance which shows how a poverty-stricken person becomes wealthy by God's grace acquired on the strength of *upasana*.

When my father was residing in the Ananta Rishi's wadi in Mumbai the story of Ganapatiboa was quite fresh in the minds of all persons residing there. When my father told the above account about Ganapatiboa to me I had begun to feel greatest respect for him. When I was in Ratnagiri I purposely went to Shirgaon to see the Ganapati temple built by Ganapatiboa. The idol of Sri Ganapati, which I saw installed in that temple is yet standing before my mental eye. And Ganapatiboa's account is yet quite fresh in my memory.

Yadneshwar Dikshit

Yadneshwar Dikshit was a spiritual preceptor of my father. Owing to his *upasana* he had achieved great divine powers. He had initiated my father into the field of *upasana* by giving him the *ekakshari mantra* of the God Sri Ganapati. The said mantra is very powerful. Dikshit has thereby conferred great obligations on our family.

While Dikshit had been travelling in the Deccan, he happened to be at Saswad in Pune district. My father was then practising there as *mukhtyar vakil*—lawyer. Dikshit had his stay there for some days. He had initiated some persons in some mantras. At that time Bhau Vithal Khaladkar was the Head Master of Marathi school in Saswad. He happened to be my father's friend. Dikshit had become his spiritual Guru by giving him some *upasana*. He had also experienced some of its wonderful effects.

Once Bhaurao, in the course of conversation said to my father, "Babasaheb, I have come to know that Yadneshwar Dikshit possesses great spiritual powers, I have become his disciple. He has initiated me in a mantra. I have seen some of its wonderful effects in a very short time. So I should like to suggest that you should also make him your Guru in spiritual matters. It will tend to your worldly and spiritual welfare."

Babasaheb accordingly went to Dikshit who initiated him with mantras in connection with Sri Ganapati and Tripurasundari. Dikshit had his stay thereafter at Saswad for nearly a month. Bhaurao master and Babasaheb daily used to go to him. Dikshit narrated to them very many pleasant incidents whereof he had experienced in his life time. They were indeed extremely wonderful.

One day my father Babasaheb was sitting near Yadneshwar Dikshit who had a rosary of rudraksha in his hand. An idea struck my father's mind that he should have such a rosary for his own use. Dikshit at once asked my father to put forth his hands, and placed his rosary on them saying, "As you are in want of a rosary, take this." He continued, "I have got this rosary from my Guru. He and I have used this for repeating our mantras amounting billions in numbers. Its efficacy is great to an extreme. I had been keeping it in my safe custody and been valuing it as my life. Keep it therefore very safe and use it for repeating your mantra. Before concluding he said my inner voice told me that you are fit for accepting this rosary and I therefore hand it over to you as *prasad*. It will undoubtedly tend to your welfare."

Babasaheb was in need of a rosary. Dikshit could read

his mind by means of his spiritual power and handed it over to him in token of his favour.

While accepting the rosary my father was convinced about his Guru's divine power of knowing what is passing in the mind of others. He also felt a sort of responsibility when he accepted the rosary. This rosary of his Guru was not like other rosaries. The Guru of Dikshit and Dikshit himself had by means of that rosary repeated their mantras amounting billions in number, it had therefore got a peculiar spiritual efficacy. A thought was therefore uppermost in his mind that he must continue repeating the mantra without break. He was immensely joyed for securing the rosary from his Guru, and he was determined to use it daily for repeating the mantra in which he was initiated by Dikshit.

Babasaheb then repeated the mantra for a countless number of times. Dikshit had informed him that in case of extreme difficulty he should repeat the mantra for a particular number of times and he will see that his difficulty will be removed. I have myself seen him having extricated from difficulty by repeating that mantra. He was courageous and calm both. He was ready to tide over any ordinary difficulty. But when any difficulty got the upper hand he would resort to this rosary and the mantra, recital of which for a particular number of times freed him from the difficult situation. I have noticed it many a time. His case apart, the use of that rosary and the mantra has given me like results several times. After demise of my father the holy rosary has been with me. I have stored the number of occasions in my memory as to when that rosary had been useful to me. This is, however, matter of pure faith. No intellectual explanation can solve occult problems.

After leaving Saswad Yadneshwar Dikshit visited some places in Maharashtra and settled at Dhar. There the Raja of that state came to know his greatness and he therefore became his disciple.

While Dikshit was passing his days at Dhar a very strange incident occurred. On one fine morning when Mrs. Dikshit got up her entire body became white from head to foot. This sudden change in colour was due to white leprosy. The Raja came to know of this and he told Dikshit that he was going to call an eminent doctor from Mumbai for treating his wife. But Dikshit was calm and quiet. He smiled at the suggestion of the Raja. "For curing my wife," he said to him, "I do not require any doctor on earth. You may arrange to send us to Saptashringi."

The Raja made all preparations for sending Dikshit and his wife to Saptashringi. Dikshit and his wife accompanied by men who were directed by the Raja to go with Dikshit, reached Saptashringi.

He fasted there for twenty-one days and offered his prayers to the presiding deity of that Shrine with reciting a mantra. On the night of the twenty first day he was told by the deity in his dream that a bath of the holy water should be given to his wife and her body will be as it was before. Accordingly she was given such a bath and when the body was rubbed by a towel, a sort of white chaff passed away from the surface of her body and its white colour totally disappeared. The white leprosy left not the least trace of it.

From the above instances any one can have the idea as

to what divine power Dikshit had possessed.

I feel the highest reverence for the mantra into which my father was originally initiated by Dikshit and subsequently I was initiated by my father. I have therefore never forgotten the directions given to me by my father regarding its proper use.

Saints Known to me

Apayya Dikshit

Apayya Dikshit lived at Shivakanchi. He was a learned man and by means of his penance accomplished spiritual attainments. He was a devotee of God Shiva. He wrote 'Kuvalayananda' a valuable treatise on Alankar Sastra. But he was more a saint than an author. On the strength of siddhis he worked astonishing miracles.

The then Maharaja of Mysore considered him as his Guru. Once, a weaver of shawls presented a very precious shawl to the Maharaja. It was woven almost with golden lace and it was therefore shining like lustrous gold. The Maharaja thought that Apayya Dikshit would be immensely pleased if he would present that shawl to him. So one day he went to Apayya Dikshit. The latter was at that time offering oblation to the fire. He called the Maharaja inside where he was engaged in fire-worship.

The Maharaja presented the shawl to Apayya Dikshit who instantaneously offered it to the fire which was in blaze in a big fire-pit. At this the Maharaja was extremely disappointed. A sad thought occurred to his mind. The precious shawl which he presented to his Guru for his personal use is now destroyed by fire. He became quite uneasy.

Apayya Dikshit could easily surmise that the Maharaja was in a dejected mood though he had no boldness to give vent to his sad thought. He asked the Maharaja to take his dinner with him to which the latter could not say *nay*.

After the dinner was over Apayya Dikshit took him to the fire place. Fire was still blazing in the big fire-pit. Apayya Dikshit removed the upper portion of the fire and caught the skirt of the shawl with pincers and lifted it up. When it got somewhat cool he held it by his hand; shook it forcibly for removing the ashes from it and threw it before the Maharaja saying, "Take your shawl. Of what use is it to me? I wonder that you yet think that the fire and I are different!"

The Maharaja was rather discomfited at this and craved for pardon. He regretted for not having known the real of his Guru. He then requested his Guru to pardon him for entertaining a narrow idea about him. Apayya Dikshit excused him for it and gave him a hearty send off.

Apayya Dikshit made a number of wonders in his life time. It is not possible to narrate all such events of his life in a small compendium. If you go to Shivakanchi you will know much about Apayya Dikshit.

Vyankatshastri Dravid

Vyankatshastri Dravid alias Shastriboa was my elder brother's spiritual Guru. He was descendant of Apayya Dikshit five degrees removed. He, by his advice, made Sardar Raste, Vishnupant Ranade contractor and many others, his disciples. When these persons had monetary difficulties they went to him and asked him as to when they will be free from them. Shastriboa would close his eyes for a minute or so and then he would declare the exact date on which they will be free from their anxiety. His prediction never came to be untrue. My brother has seen such things taking place off and on.

My elder brother the late of Gangadhar alias Tatyasaheb Kher was a teacher in the New English School Pune. He graduated in 1890 and wanted to keep terms for LL.B. at Mumbai. He had therefore applied to the Director of Public

Instruction saying that he should be given a post of a Teacher in the Elphinston High School Mumbai. He had attached to his application true certificates about his efficiency given to him by Principal Selby of the Deccan College and Principal Apte of the Fergusson College Pune. There was no reply to it for upwards a week and therefore he went to Shastriboa for asking him the reason of delay in getting a reply to his application.

Shastriboa told him that the director Mr. Chatfield has come to a decision to appoint you as a teacher in the Elphinston High School, but he has not yet decided as to what amount of pay should be sanctioned. By deciding this, he will sign the order on the 8th day and the scale of his pay will be a little bit higher than others.

It was exactly on the 8th day the director signed the order appointing my brother as a teacher in the Elphinston High School on a monthly salary of Rs.60. It was worthwhile noting in this connection that a B.A. in those days was first appointed on Rs.45 a month and an M.A. was appointed on Rs.60 a month. My brother was B.A. still he was appointed on Rs.60. The higher salary was given to him by virtue of the excellent certificates given to him by the principals of two colleges. The other teachers in the department made complaints about the higher salary given to my bother but the director set the complaints at rest by saying that the ordinary scale had been deviated in the case of my brother because of his efficiency.

Shastriboa had advised my brother to worship the God Shiva with a certain mantra. He acted up to his advice till his life's end which took place when he was 89 years old. He also possessed certain spiritual power on the strength of his *upasana*.

When my brother was a teacher in the New English School at Pune, Mr. Panse was the Persian language teacher in the same school. Both of them were intimate friends. But both of them were at two opposite extremities in religious matters. My brother believed in God while Panse was atheist.

Once Mr. Panse's brother-in-law was in extreme difficulty and Mr. Panse had given him a loan of Rs.1200. Mr. Panse had borrowed this from a money-lender for helping his brother-in-law. The brother-in-law went on giving promises after promises that he would return the amount on certain date. But money was not forthcoming and Mr. Panse was being hardly pressed by the money-lender to return the amount which he had borrowed from him. In this way nearly four months passed away. Mr. Panse was in a fix.

As already said above Mr. Panse was an atheist. He had no good opinion about saints. He told my brother about the above transaction and how he had been in awkward position on that account. My brother asked him to accompany him to Shastriboa's house and place his grievance before him. He will tell you the date on which your anxiety will be removed. Mr. Panse asked my brother whether any amount of money would have to be paid to him. My brother replied, "Even if you pay him any amount he would not accept it."

"If it is so, I shall accompany you," said Mr. Panse. "On any day you appoint. But I have not the least faith on such people."

"There is no question of your faith in the case of my

Guru."

Shastriboa dealt with such questions only on Tuesdays and Fridays as he was a devotee of Sri Jagadamba and the above days are consecrated to that Goddess. My brother therefore took Mr. Panse to Shastriboa on a certain Tuesday. Mr. Panse explained the purpose of his visit. At this Shastriboa kept his eyes closed for nearly for five minutes and then opened them. Then he said to Mr. Panse, "Your brother-in-law will pay you Rs.700 on coming Friday."

Mr. Panse then asked him about the rest of the amount to which Shastriboa said, "After you get 700 rupees I shall consider about the remaining amount."

Mr. Panse anxiously kept waiting the arrival of Friday. At last the Friday came. At abut 7 or 8 in the morning the father-in-law of his sister came to him and paid 700 rupees to him. Shastriboa's word came to be true.

Mr. Panse thought that Shastriboa must have had some supernatural power. Then he asked Shastriboa about the remaining amount. He also named the day on which Mr. Panse would receive the amount. That amount was also received on that particular day.

These events made Mr. Panse feel the highest respect for Shastriboa. He was at first an atheist but he was totally changed. He thought that some higher powers must be existing and they must have been guiding the destinies of man. He then became a disciple of Shastriboa and he daily used to repeat the mantra into which he was initiated by Shastriboa.

I always used to see Shastriboa; his bright and grand personality yet stands before my mental eye. His figure was nearly seven feet tall. I have scarcely seen such a person in my life time. He held a big circular mark of *kumkum* on his forehead. He wore simple clothes according to the fashions of those times.

I am an eyewitness to the incidents narrated above. After completing 6th standard in the New English School at Pune, I went to Mumbai and joined the Elphinston in the Matriculation class. My brother had already gone there a year before. Our two or three years may have passed when we heard about the death of Shastriboa. We grieved his loss very much as it was hard to find any other man endowed with such spiritual power.

Now I place before the reader the information about some yogis who had obtained many *siddhis* by practicing yoga. On the strength of *siddhis* they worked wonders, but their lives rest in oblivion. In jungles far away from human habitation fragrant flowers blow and the whole atmosphere is filled with their fragrance but there is no human being to enjoy it. As those flowers blow in solitude, they fade in it, unseen by any one. Such is the life of some great persons. Similar was the life of yogi's I am just describing. None knew where and when they came to the place where they settled. They shined after some person came in contact with them.

Avaliya of Chilavadi

The story of this yogi was told by Sambhajinana, Head Master of Karjat Marathi School some fifty years back. He was a contemporary of this great yogi and he had first hand information about his mode of life and miracles he performed. Sambhaji Nana was my intimate friend and he was most reliable.

Chilavadi is in Karjat Taluka of Ahmednagar District. It is about five miles distant from Rashin, another village in the same Taluka. Just half way between these two villages this yogi Avaliya was residing in a hut. It was just facing the passage between these two villages. In front of this hut there was a spacious courtyard where some animals like cow, bullocks, dogs, cats, rats etcetera had made their resting place. Here, dogs, cats, and rats were seen having abandoned their natural antipathy and playing with one another joyfully without hurting it anywise. The passers-by were struck with wonder by witnessing this unnatural phenomenon. It was generally supposed that animals belonged to the yogi.

Any wayfarers, while passing this way used to call this yogi and asked him how he fared. As soon as there was such a called the yogi said *aadaab*. When questioned as to what he was doing he said that he was cooking though he was sitting at ease and doing nothing. There was one hearth in that hut. Two pieces of wood were placed in it crosswise one above the other. But none found them ever kindled nor was found fire in the hearth. There was empty pot always kept in the hearth. The Avaliya was also never seen eating anything by any one.

Sometimes a man entered his hut and said he was hungry. The Avaliya asked him to put his hand in any one of the earthen pot which were placed upon one another in one of the corners of that hut. When that man put his hand into one of them he found some eatables to satisfy his hunger. How those articles came there none knew. The Avaliya never went out leaving his hut to purchase them nor did he accept either money or such articles from any one. It was therefore a mystery that such eatables should be found in the earthen pots. At any other times these pots were quite empty. I was told that many persons had found sweets, ground-nuts, fried grams etc. in these pots.

Once, a man was passing by the hut. Sun was very hot in summer and he felt very thirsty. He entered the hut and asked the Avaliya if he would get water to drink. The Avaliya said that he was sorry as there was no water in the hut. He however said that if the man would dig the ground just near the hut he would get the water. As the level of the ground was somewhat high he thought that unless he dug a pit 20 or 30 feet deep there was not the least chance of finding water. He therefore thought that the Avaliya asking him to dig the ground near his hut was merely joking. The Avaliya again pressed him to dig the ground. In response he dug the ground to the depth of nearly a foot and a half, he, to a great surprise found that a crystal clear stream of water rushed into the pit. In a minute the pit was half full with water. He quenched his thirst and went away. That spring of water was an object of wonder to those that passed by this way. The history about this stream of water was known to those at Rashin, Chilavadi and also to some at Karjat.

Sambhajinana who told me the above incidents and his own experience, was the *Kulkarni* of Chilavadi. Sometimes he was required to go to that village from Rashin. He had his own house at Rashin where he had kept his family

Once he happened to return from Chilavadi late in the evening. It was then rainy season. After he left Chilavadi rain began to pour in torrents. The result was that he could not see the way under his feet as rain water thereon was knee deep. He had no umbrella; his clothes were all drenched in water. His body began to shiver owing to the cold blasts of winds were blowing along with the rain. In these circumstances he anyhow came near the hut of avaliya. Sambhajinana called him. The Avaliya uttered the word *aadaab*. "Nana," said he in a tone of surprise as he saw Nana, "is this a time to be out?"

To this Nana replied, "I left Chilavadi when there were no signs of rain though the sky was somewhat cloudy.

But soon after that there was a storm followed by copious rainfall. I thought I could easily go to Rashin. But my expectation proved a failure and anyhow I reached your hut."

By this time rain had almost stopped.

The Avaliya called two bullocks by their names. The bullocks stout and strong came at once before the Avaliya. To them he said that they should go with Nana as far as the entrance of Rashin and then return. He asked Nana to go with the bullocks. While Nana was going two bullocks were walking on either side of him. When Nana reached the gateway of Rashin they returned and went to the place of their resort.

When this Avaliya died, all the animals in the open courtyard were sitting with their faces downwards and moaning their master's loss by shedding tears in their eyes. Their tears were trickling on the ground. People of Chilavadi and Rashin went there for paying the Avaliya their last visit and made arrangement for his burial and returned after burial to their respective villages with heavy hearts. The stock of animals only remained there. Then the Kulkarni of the village reported to the *mamledar* of Karjat that the Avaliya was dead leaving his animals behind him and that orders may be issued as to what should be done as there was no heir to the *avaliya*. The *mamledar* directed him to make investigation of the animals and that they should be sent to the Taluka town along with the report. They were, according to the law, to be sold by auction and the sale proceeds were to be credited to Government.

The *Patil* and *Kulkarni* went to the place where those

animals were, but not a single animal was found there. Naturally no investigation was done.

The Kulkarni made a report to the *mamledar* that no animal could be traced there. All of them had disappeared at night, upon this the *mamledar* went to Rashin and personally made inquiries but no one could say how the animals disappeared and whereto they had gone. None could find any explanation about them. Some, however, conjectured that the *avaliya* must have by his power created merely a vision in respect of these animals.

Sheikh Mohammad

The above Muslim saint was a resident of Srigonda, a Taluka place in the District of Ahmednagar. He was a devotee of Sri Ganesh, God of the Hindus. He was also a yogi. The Moraya Gosavi of Chinchwad, a well known saint in Pune district and Jayram Swami a saint from Satara district and some other saints were his contemporaries. Sheikh Mohammad's Guru was a Brahmin by caste. It was he who directed Sheikh Mohammad to worship Sri Ganesh. Sheikh Mohammad was an excellent Marathi writer. 'Yoga Sangram' is written by him in Marathi. It was printed and published; some years ago.

According to the direction of his Guru, Sheikh Mohammad continued worshipping Sri Ganesh with great zeal. Once he was sitting in meditation on a slab of stone in a jungle for twenty one days without food or drink. On the 19th day a ferocious tiger appeared before him. But he said to Ganesh that he did not wish to see him in the form of a tiger. He therefore asked the tiger to walk away. On the next day a big cobra appeared before him. This time also he commanded the cobra to go away from him as he wanted to see Sri Ganesh; and on the 21st day of his meditation Sri Ganesh appeared before him and then he left the slab of stone.

After gaining spiritual powers he was performing *kirtans*. When he was dealing with a certain topic, he abruptly cried aloud, and rubbed both the palms of his hands. The audience asked him the reason of rubbing his palms. Sheikh Mohammad said, "Jayram Swami was doing *kirtan* in a shade erected for the purpose at Vadgaon in Satara district. All were engrossed in listening to his oration, when the covering of the shade caught fire by the flame of the torch. None took heed of it. So I went there and extinguished the fire by means of my palms." So saying he showed his palms to the preassembled. The hands were coal-black.

Some people got information from Vadgaon out of curiosity to ascertain whether Sheikh Mohammed's word was true. Vadgaon people informed that the upper covering of the shade had really caught fire but it got automatically extinguished.

Once, an officer on tour forced Sheikh Mohammed to carry his office box. Sheikh Mohammad was carrying it on his head. The Officer's subordinate was walking with him. Sheikh Mohammed while walking with a load on his head went into trance. The box was no more on his head. He was walking on the ground and the box was moving ahead one foot in the air above his head. The officer noticed with surprise the box moving in the air without any support. He supposed that Sheikh Mohammad must be an extraordinary person. He therefore fell at his feet begged to be forgiven for forcing him to carry his box.

Once, Sheikh Mohammad went to Chinchwad. He stood at the door of Moraya Gosavi who was also a great saint. He asked for alms. Flour was served in a bowl. But he said that he wanted the bowl to be filled to the brim. Therefore more flour was put into it for filling but it could not be full. At last a small girl put her handful of flour into it and the bowl was overfull. The doorkeeper thought it strange occurrence, and he reported the matter to Moraya Gosavi. He came out but the person begging alms could not be seen. He therefore went out and found him out at some distance. They recognised each other.

Moraya Gosavi asked, "When did you come?"

"I came when you were worshipping Sri Ganapati in your mind." Sheikh Mohammad replied. "You were garlanding the God but the garland was entangled. I came at that time when you were engaged in untying the knots of the garland."

Sheikh Mohammad just alluded to the fact which actually had taken place when Moraya Gosavi was worshipping Sri Ganapati in his mind. Then Moraya Gosavi took him to his abode for dinner. After dinner and conversation Sheikh Mohammed started for his village.

In one *abhanga* he has stated, "We are Brahmins by caste but our relatives are Muslims."

His tomb is built in Srigonda. It is worshipped by Hindus and Muslims both. Both have equal respect for this saint.

134 Saints Known to me

Mamdya Vedaa

The above person was a yogi and *dnyani*. But looked like a madman. Hence he was called Mamdya *Vedaa*. Many persons might have seen him begging at Srigonda, some sixty five years back. But none was aware of his greatness as a yogi. He was always calm, quiet and contended. He never gave trouble to any one nor did anybody ever give him trouble.

One Balaboa Agnihotri went to see the Maharaj of Akkalkot who was a great saint. When he fell at the feet of the Maharaj, the latter said to him, "Why did you come to me? Go to Mamdya of your village and make a bow to him."

Balaboa returned by railway train and got down at Pimpri station which is four miles distant from Srigonda. When he came out of the station, Mamdya stood before him. He asked Balaboa "Did you see the Maharaj of Akkalkot?"

Balaboa said, "Yes I did, but he had told me to see you."

At this Mamdya only smiled. Balboa came to Srigonda in a *tonga*—horse-carriage, which was ahead of all other *tongas* and reaches Srigonda first. As soon as Balaboa alighted fro the *tonga*, Mamdya was again standing before him. Balboa fell at his feet. He was convinced that Mamdya was not mad but he was a saint.

This account was given to me by Balaboa himself.

Keshavboa Yevalekar

Nearly seventy five years passed away since one Mr. Deshpande was *shirastedar* in the District Judge's court at Nasik, on a monthly salary of Rs.150. He had an only son by name Keshav. Mr. Deshpande and his wife were both pious and they had firm faith in God. Keshav, from his boyhood took a liking for devotion to the God Sri Dattatray. He daily used to worship him with flowers brought by himself. When he completed his Marathi education he was sent to English School in Pune. There also he was worshipping his chosen deity. Mr. Deshpande used to send him Rs.25 every month with a view that his son should live comfortably. Some students in his class were very poor. He did not like that he should live in comfort and they should be in distress. He therefore distributed major portion of the amount amongst the needy friends and he himself lived on alms. Thus he helped the promising friends in his class.

His father came to know that Keshav was spending the money in the above way and he himself begs along with his poor friends.

He questioned his son, "Do you beg?" On getting an affirmative answer, he further asked, "Then what do you do about hotel charges, the money I send you?"

"I pay that amount to poor boys." was a reply. His father did not ask him any further question. He was then in Matriculation class.

Mr. Deshpande and his wife wished to get their son married. But Keshav plainly told them that he did not wish to marry, as he desired to spend some days in some holy place to secure peace of mind.

So saying he left home and went on visiting holy places. While so travelling he happened to meet Brahmendra swami and made him his Guru in spiritual matters. This swami was the Guru of Jayajirao Shinde of Gwalior.

We shall hereafter call Keshav as Keshavboa. He travelled all over India on foot twice or thrice, with a view to visit all holy places. In these travels he never took the help or any conveyance. He travelled over vast tracts in India and the Himalayas with his Guru Brahmendra Swami. He had gone even to Manas Lake with him. He sometimes gave graphic description on his travels.

I have seen his Guru Brahmendra Swami when he had been at Poona for installing the idol of Sri Dattatray in Rasta Peth. He was called for dinner by my father. When he was asked what his age was he said that he was then 115 years of age. From his appearance he seemed to be of that age; though his health was quite sound, figure grand.

Keshavboa while travelling in the Himalayas learnt to prepare gold from copper. But he used it for benevolent purpose.

Keshavboa never accepted even a pie from others. He used to come to my father at Jamkhed in Ahmednagar District. When he came, he used to have his stay with us for two or three months. During his stay, he used to go into the jungle every second or third week and prepare an ingot of gold from copper. He used to return from the jungle after two or three days. Then he use to hand over that ingot of gold-result or alchemy to one of his disciples for selling it in the market. The disciple would sell that piece of gold and would get nearly two rupees less than the rate of pure gold. He used to spent that amount for giving a dinner to seven or eight hundred persons of all castes. Every second or third week such a dinner was being given to the people. He gave hundreds of such dinners in his life time, on the strength of alchemy.

In the course of conversation he told me that for turning copper into gold he made use of the creeper by name *chandravalli*. These creepers abound in the Himalayas. In our jungles in the Deccan they are found somewhere but they are rare. He said that he had planted these creepers on the Sri Shailya Mountain, and that he would acquaint with that process.

There was a notion rite among elderly persons that turning copper into gold by the process of alchemy totally annihilates one's progeny. And therefore I never hankered after being rich by alchemy. When Keshavboa came to us that topic was revived but when he went away from us we forgot it altogether.

In a division suit Keshavboa got twelve thousand rupees to his shares. Out of this amount he built a Dattatray Mandir and the remaining amount was kept in the name of a trustee for continuing the daily worship of the idol in that shrine and for other necessary expenses. Then again he went on travelling and in the midst of his travels his life ended about 62 years back.

Dev Mamledar

The above named saint was well known to the people of Maharashtra. He was also otherwise called Yashwantrao Maharaj. He was a great favourite of God. His motto was never to tell a lie under any circumstances. And he had got the fruit of his truth speaking. His prediction always came to be true. He held the post of a *mamledar* in the British Regime. He never dishonoured any guest. On the other hand he thought that it was his duty to treat the guest most hospitably. Owing to his philanthropic nature crowds of *gosavis, bairagis*—sages, yogis and the like haunted his home off and on. But he never failed to give them food etc and turn them disappointed.

Once he had no money to treat such people. He was therefore in a great fix. He told his head clerk that he would draw five hundred rupees from the Government treasury and that he would return the amount as soon as he had it from any other source.

The head clerk said, "Rao sahib, if the Collector or any other superior officer happens to know this, I shall be prosecuted for misappropriating Government money."

The Mamledar replied, "You need not be in anyways anxious about it. I shall look to it."

So saying the Mamledar drew Rs. 500 and gave dinner to the *bairagis* and *gosavis*.

On the other hand the head clerk made a detailed report to the Collector stating all the above facts. The Collector read the report and without losing any time paid a surprise visit to the *taluka* town for inspecting the treasury. He called the head clerk and in his presence he counted the money in the Government treasury. Not a single pie came less than the previous day's statement submitted to the Deputy Collector.

The Collector then asked an explanation from the Head clerk as to why he made a false report.

The Head clerk averred with confidence that his report was correct and true. The Collector may, if he chose, ask the Mamledar about the same matter.

The Collector accordingly saw the Mamledar and asked him if he took five hundred rupees from the treasury for feeding the *bairagis*. The Mamledar said that he appropriated Government money for that purpose as he himself was short of money and that the report of Head clerk was true. "Did you then replace the amount in the treasury?" was the Collector's next question.

The Mamledar answered in the negative and said that

Saints known to me 143

he was shortly going to replace it.

Hearing this, the Collector was greatly wonder struck. The Mamledar says that he did not recoup the amount; whereas in the treasury there was not a *paisa* less. These things were beyond explanation. Who paid the amount into the treasury and when? None could solve this strange problem. Every one said that the God Pandurang himself must have come to the help of the Mamledar and he must have paid the amount into the treasury as he had run to the help of Damajipant of Mangalvedha in the garb of Vithu Mahar and paid for him the amount due to the *badshaha* and got his receipt.

When Yashwantrao Maharaj was a *mamledar* at Satana in Nasik district, the commissioner of Nasik went there for office inspection. The commissioner's horse suddenly got seriously ill and was on the point of death. His peon told him that the ashes given by Dev Mamledar, if applied to the body of the horse, he would be immediately cured. The peon came to the Mamledar and told him the horse of the Commissioner was serious and that he wanted ashes from him for curing the horse. The Mamledar gave him ashes and told him that they should be applied to the body of the horse.

As soon as the ashes were applied to the body of the horse he got up and began to eat grass. He was free from ailment. The peon told all this to the Commissioner. He invited the Mamledar to his tent and thanked him for curing his horse. That officer asked the Mamledar as to what he should do for him for requiting his favour. The Mamledar said, "People impound dumb animals in the cattle pound. They are poorly fed there. I wish that they should be freed from their distressful condition. My request therefore is that the Cattle Trespass Act should be abolished."

The commissioner said, "Well it is not within my power to cancel the Act passed by the legislature but I shall try to suspend its operation in a taluka where you will be posted as Mamledar." The Commissioner then got Government permission for such suspension. Thereafter the operation of the act was suspended by the resolution of Government in the taluka where Yashwantrao Maharaj worked as Mamledar.

After he retired from Government service, once he came to Pune. He had his stay in Godbole wada in red Jogeshwari lane. It was just in front of your house. Crowds of people were coming to see this *mahatma*—great holy man. A woman presented her nose ring of pearls to him. She had in her mind that she would give her nose ring to Dev Mamledar in case a son would be born to her. And she having had a son had presented the nose ring to Dev Mamledar. When her husband knew this he scolded her and at once went to Dev Mamledar. He said to the Mamledar, "You are a cheat; you rob other's wives of their ornaments!"

The Mamledar asked him, "Why are you angry with me? How have I offended you?"

The husband of the woman said, "You have usurped the nose ring of my wife."

The Mamledar told him that he knew nothing about the nose ring.

While this conversation was going on, one man placed a cocoa-nut before the Mamledar and fell at his feet. The later asked him to break the cocoanut. The man broke it and to the surprise of all a nose ring came out of it. The Mamledar asked the woman's husband to see it whether it belonged to him and if so to take it away.

He recognized his nose ring but he was at a loss to know how it came out of the cocoanut. He was astounded to see it. He could not know what to speak. He begged the Mamledar to be pardoned for using bad words to him. Without touching the nose ring he went away. This wonderful event was then widely known to the people in Pune at that time.

In his last days Dev Mamledar told his wife that his life's end was very near and that if she wished to accompany him she would not get salvation. He further said, "If you remain one year after I pass away for good, you will not get another birth; so it will be better for you to wait a year after my departure."

Dev Mamledar died on *Margashirsha shudh ekadashi* and his wife passed away exactly a year after him, according to his prediction.

Vithoba Anna Karhadkar

History of this saint was narrated to me by my father sixty five years ago. I am stating it as I was told.

Vithoba Anna's disciples were many in number. Once he was going to *Konkan* accompanied by nearly fifty of them. All of them came to Sahyadri *ghat*. The party was travelling on foot, when they heard a loud cry of a tiger. At this the disciples were frightened and they took resort to branches on tall trees for protection. Vithoba Anna however sat on a slab of stone on the ground. He seemed quite unmoved by tiger's cry. In the meantime the tiger seemed to be coming in the direction where Vithoba Anna had taken his seat. The tiger was limping. Vithoba Anna called him saying, 'Let me see why you are limping.' The tiger approached him and stood there as if he was tamed. The disciples thought that the tiger would not leave their

Guru alive.

Vithoba Anna took the tiger's paw in his own hand. He saw that a big thorn was broken in it and hence the beast was limping. This whole affair was so peacefully going on that it appeared that a doctor was examining a human patient. Vithoba Anna took out from his purse, a needle, a forceps and a marking nut. With the help of needle and forceps he extracted the thorn out of the tigers paw; applied oil of the marking nut to the portion of the paw wherefrom the thorn was extracted and fomented it by fire kindled for the purpose. When the tiger had a pang at the time of fomentation he forcibly drew back his paw from Vithoba Anna's hand. But again he placed his paw into Anna's hand for treatment.

When the treatment was over, Anna patted the tiger's back and said to him, "Now you may go! You will be alright very soon." The tiger seemed as if he understood what Anna said and he started from there. He was looking at Vithoba Anna till he went nearly ten or twelve paces. He then gave a loud cry and disappeared in the thicket of trees.

As long as the disciples were observing the above procedure, they were struck dumb and they had no hopes about their Guru, for they had not known his power till then. Strictly maintaining the vow of Ahimsa gives such a power to a man. Patanjali says that when such a power is cultivated by any person, any one who comes near such a person never feel enmity against him. Owing to the cultivation of such a power by Vithoba Anna the tiger was calm and quiet in his presence. He had totally abandoned his natural ferocious nature.

APPENDIX

The powers which a man acquires by Karma, Bhakti and Dnyan are due to the elevation of soul. But some persons achieve some like powers by virtue of Saabari Mantras. I am here describing some such instances about which I have reliable information. I myself have seen some wonderful feats made by them.

APPENDIX

Kashirao Baba

Some seventy five years back my father was a clerk in Pune Collector's office. At that time one great *mantrik* Kashirao Baba had come to Pune from Deccan Hyderabad. On a certain night he was going to exhibit his powers gained by him by means of *saabari* mantras. My father having been invited had gone to see the programme. A large number of persons was present there.

Kashirao Baba commenced his performance. He covered his whole body below neck with a large piece of cloth. Then he said to the person assembled, "First of all I am thinking of distributing *pan-supari* to you."

All the persons were listening to him with a curiosity and anxiously looking to what he was going to do.

In the meanwhile some object, the height of which was nearly a foot and a half, seemed to have sprung inside the cloth which covered Baba's body. Baba told a person nearby to take out that object. He did so... The object so drawn out was a basket containing nearly three thousand ripe betel leaves. They were well arranged in the basket. Similarly Baba produced betel nuts, scented tobacco and other articles required for chewing. He distributed *pan-supari* to all. Half an hour was spent in doing this.

Baba then told the person to state what they wanted and that he would produce it as soon as they named it.

Some persons said, "We want Khichadi to eat."

Baba closed his eyes for nearly five minutes and asked one of them to take a pot from within his covering. It was a pot containing Khichadi! Baba said, "You may eat it if you like, but I have brought it from an untouchable's house. If you do not want it I shall return it to its owner."

The pot was given to Baba who took it inside the cloth which enveloped him and the pot disappeared.

Then a man came before Baba. He said, "I am expecting an important letter by tomorrow morning's post. I wish therefore to know whether the letter has arrived here in the post office."

Baba said that the letter has arrived; he asked the man whether he wanted to see it.

"It will be better if I can see it now," said the man.

Baba took it out from the inside of his covering and threw it before the said person. The letter did not bear the stamp of Pune post office. After the man was convinced about the expected letter Baba demanded it back for restoring it to its proper place in the post office. He received the letter from the man, hid it under the covering of his body. The letter disappeared from it!

After he made certain other performances, his last performance made the assemblage highly surprised and frightened too.

Among the spectators was the Deputy Collector of Pune. He had in his charge the Government treasury.

Kashirao Baba asked the Deputy Collector whether he should produce money bags from the government treasury. The Deputy Collector was in-charge of the government treasury. He thought that Kashirao Baba must be merely joking. He, therefore, asked him to produce them. There were twenty bags containing forty thousand rupees in a room with a double lock. They were all sealed by the officer in charge of the treasury. The Deputy Collector was quite sure that those bags could not be removed from the iron bars of the room.

Being very sure that it was quite impossible to carry money bags from the treasury room, The Deputy Collector boldly told Kashirao Baba to bring the bags. He still thought that Baba was joking.

Baba said, "Why should I joke? If you wish I shall bring all the bags here before you."

"I say bring them," replied the Deputy Collector. "Sit in front of me and drag the bags out one by one from inside my covering garment," said Baba.

Baba then placed all the sealed bags before the spectators. At this the Deputy Collector was struck with terror. He thought, 'If superior officers chance to know this, what would be the consequences? Perhaps I may be dismissed; nay, even prosecuted.' He repented for telling Baba to produce the money bags. But repentance was of no avail now.

Out of the twenty bags nineteen were returned to the treasury, and Baba broke open the seal of the remaining bag and opened it. He distributed all the rupees from that bag to many persons and told them to return the amount the next morning so that he might send it back to the treasury. "Otherwise," he said, "the treasury officer would be prosecuted for misappropriating government money, and he would be jailed."

The persons to whom the amount was given went home and kept it safe, as they had to return it the next morning. When Baba distributed the amount the treasury officer was at a loss to know what he should do under those circumstances. All the spectators being highly surprised by the performance had also gone to their homes. Next morning the persons to whom Baba had paid money indiscriminately found that the money had disappeared from the places where they had placed it.

The treasury officer went to his office very early in the morning and opened the treasury room. He found all the twenty bags sealed as before. They too in double lock. The double locks were intact. The treasury officer did not notice the least change in the previous situation. He felt great relief and was fully convinced about the powers of Baba.

It must be noted that Kashirao Baba had obtained these powers by means of *saabari mantras*. They are considered as minor ones. The power gained by yoga, *bhakti*—devotion—etcetera as denoted by Bhagavad-Gita, are highly important as they tend to man's salvation.

Jaglya of Bhingar

There was a Jaglya at Bhingar a small town nearly a couple of miles from Ahmednagar. He knew a mantra by which he removed the pangs of anyone caused by scorpion-bite. If any person was suffering from scorpion bite, any other person might go to this Jaglya and inform him that such and such a man was so suffering.

The Jaglya would only say, "The man suffering was not bitten, but the scorpion bit you."

At this the informant would begin to have real pangs. The man about whom the information was given would then be completely cured. Then the Jaglya would say to the informant, "You are not bitten but the stepping stone of the *Chavadi* was bitten."

As soon as Jaglya said so the informant would be cured and a small piece of stone was dislocated from the stepping stone with a noise as if was removed by a chisel.

We had a friend in Bhingar who was a teacher in girl's school at Karjat in Ahmednagar District. He offered the Jaglya any amount of money for securing the said mantra but he did not part with it. He did not even acquaint any one with it.

At last the mantra died with the Jaglya.

Mehetar of Daund

Once I came to Daund from Mumbai at about 8am in the morning. There was four hours time for starting a train for Ahmednagar. I had to go by that train. Dr. Sailu Sayanna was incharge of government dispensary at Daund and as he was my friend I went to see him in the dispensary, which was very near the railway station. Both of us were talking together. In the meantime we heard a very loud cry rose in the Railway Station. I went to the station building to see what the consternation was due to. The people assembled there were saying that a big cobra had gone into the heap of stones. One of the men said that the Mehetar should be called there without delay.

Within a short time Mehetar arrived on the spot. He asked the persons there as to where the cobra was. They replied that it had entered the heap of stones. Mehetar went near the heap of stones and asked the cobra to come out of that heap.

No sooner did he say so the cobra came out of the heap of stones and stood near Mehetar. Its length was nearly six feet and it was as big as a man's arm. Mehetar caught it. He wound it round about his elbow and shoulder just like a rope and crossing the bridge he went to the other side of the station. I followed him along with many other spectators. Mehetar got down the staircase and in front of it he spread some sand on four sides to mark the boundary. The space covered thereby was merely 7 feet by 7 feet. He placed the cobra in that square and took his departure from there.

We spectators tarried there for nearly three fourth of an hour to see the movements of that creature. It was freely crawling in that square, but as soon as it went near the boundary-line it shrank back as if startled. It could not cross any of the four boundary lines of the square. Its movements were confined only to the place covered by the square. I was, in fact, astounded to see it.

As the time to leave Daund by train was approaching, I came back to the station. There I learnt that Mehetar was a magician of great order.

On the other occasion I was going from Daund to Mumbai. The same Mehetar entered the compartment in which I had taken my seat. He came and took his seat by my side. I recognized him. He was the same Mehetar who had confined the great cobra near the staircase at Daund. I therefore at once questioned him, "Are you the Mehetar of Daund?"

"Yes," he said and questioned me in return, "How do you know me?"

Then I referred to the incident of cobra which took place a few days ago. I then asked him, "How did you handle that dangerous creature just like a rope?"

He said, "I do all these things by means of mantras. I can thus make an inanimate thing like a table walk on its four feet; produce any article named by any person etcetera, on the strength of mantras."

I asked him, "Will you please do some such thing to satisfy our curiosity?"

He then took a *paisa* from me. He asked me to put in

initials on it. I did it with end of my sharp knife. He then asked me to throw that *paisa* out of the running train. Accordingly I went near the window and threw the *paisa* down. I heard its noise when it fell forcibly on the rock below. I then resumed my seat to see what would happen further.

A man was sitting on my right side. Mehetar charged him for taking my *paisa* and hiding it in his cap. He lifted the cap from his head and the *paisa* fell down from the cap! I saw it and to my surprise I found that it was the same *paisa* which I threw out of the train as it had my own initials carved thereon. All the passengers in our compartment were amazed at this performance.

The mantrik

Some years back a *mantrik* had come to Ahmednagar. His programme was arranged by some men. Many persons were present to witness it. First the *mantrik* produced some articles as suggested by certain persons. In the end he told the spectators that a procession of scorpions would soon be marching before them. They should therefore keep a clear passage—a foot and a half wide—for their march from one wall of the hall to the other.

The spectators made such a passage. The *mantrik* then gave a hint to the scorpions to start their march.

Immediately a small crust of a wall fell on the ground, producing a hole in it. Scorpions began to come out of that hole and pass by the way previously cleared for them. They came one after another and entered a hole in the opposite wall. Thus the scorpions were coming from one wall and disappearing in the opposite one. The march was going on for nearly five minutes. Seeing the line of scorpions the spectators were rather struck with terror but the *mantrik* asked them to be quiet and he assured them that no scorpion would hurt them.

In that procession there were scorpions of various sizes and colours. Commonly the greatest length of a big scorpion is generally two inches and a half. But in the procession some of them were even seven or eight inches in length. As to their colour, some were white, some red and some coal-black.

The *mantrik* then said, "Now the king of these scorpions will come out of the hole."

Immediately a big white scorpion issued from the hole. It was followed by nearly fifteen such scorpions. All of them marched towards the hole in the opposite wall and disappeared in it.

This awe-inspiring and frightful spectacle had struck the spectators with terror but when scorpion's march ended, they heaved a sigh of relief.

* * *

UPCOMING TITLES

SHASTRI - *Amrutaputra*
B. D. Kher
A Biographical novel on the life of Lal Bahadur Shastri

Ocean of God Particles
Rajendra Kher
Philosophical fiction

A Tale of Two Kingdoms
Rajendra Kher
A Udayan-Vasavdatta Story

Road to self realization
Rajendra Kher
Secrets behind Subjective Idol Worship

Empire of God
Rajendra Kher
Were God astronauts?

contact:
Vihang Publications
E-mail: vihangpublications@gmail.com
www.vihangpublications.com

Saints known to me 161

www.ingramcontent.com/pod-product-compliance
Lightning Source LLC
Chambersburg PA
CBHW071507040426
42444CB00008B/1526